CHAPPELLI
THE CUTTING EDGE

CHAPPELLI
THE CUTTING EDGE

Ian Chappell

Foreword by Sir Garry Sobers

SWAN
PUBLISHING

First published in 1992 by
Swan Publishing Pty Ltd
P.O. Box 577, Nedlands, W.A. 6009

National Library of Australia
Cataloguing-in-Publication data.

Chappell, Ian, 1943 – .
Chappelli—The Cutting Edge.

ISBN 0 646 10665 1.

1. Cricket – Australia – History.
I. Title.

796.3580994

Printed in Australia by The Book Printer

Designer: Stan Lamond, Lamond Art & Design

CONTENTS

FOREWORD

by Sir Garry Sobers

A cricket book by Ian Chappell is like one of his innings, positive, dynamic and thoroughly entertaining. He attacks the bad points he believes afflict the game with the same gusto with which he would despatch a bad ball. His suggestions for improvement are made with the boldness he had in his strokeplay. His approach to writing is very much what it was to batting, powerful and no-nonsense.

Cricket has been Ian Chappell's life. Born into a family with strong cricketing links, his grandfather was the legendary Vic Richardson, whose footsteps he followed as Australian Test captain. Throughout these pages, it is obvious that cricket has also been Ian Chappell's passion.

I've known Ian since he was a teenager and I was playing for South Australia in the Sheffield Shield in the early 1960s. Quiet, perhaps a little shy in those days, I remember him sticking around the senior players in the State side, learning what he could from listening and watching. He got his first match for the state late in 1962 when he took my place, as I had to return home for a Test series against India. It was the start of a career in which he developed into one of Australia's finest attacking batsmen and a captain I rate the best I've played against.

We played several times with and against each other and were rival captains in the series between the Rest of the World team and Australia in the 1971-72 season. It was one of the most enjoyable series I've played in, mainly because our approach to the game was so similar. Our first priority was to win and we were both willing to take chances to achieve that end. It was an example our players followed and it made for wonderful cricket.

I wasn't in the least surprised when he picked the Australian team out of a slump and moulded it into the strongest combination in Test cricket. The welfare of his players was always of paramount importance to him, and he earned both their respect and their loyalty, so vital in leadership of any kind. Inevitably, this brought him into conflict with the administrators with whom he fought many running battles. As is evident, his attitude to the establishment has changed little through the years, not without reason.

He covers a widc range of topics in these pages and, even if I don't agree with all his points, they are all thought-provoking. In many cases, he is advancing the views of present-day players and fans. The administrators, at all levels, would do well to examine them carefully.

For a start, they could look at their 'one bouncer per batsman per over' regulation. I am completely against the repeated tampering with the laws, and this is surely one of the most ludicrous and unnecessary changes they have come up with. Ian Chappell strongly condemns it in the same way that every other cricketer I've heard on the subject does. So why is it still in place?

Ian also raises the issue of the power of the veto that England and Australia still maintain at the International Cricket Council (ICC). It is obviously a throwback to colonialism and, as he points out, causes resentment in an organization that should, in this day and age, be completely democratic. The West Indies Board has put forward a resolution to have it scrapped but, like most things at that level, it has been deferred.

One of his main concerns is for the future of Test cricket in the modern era. Typically, he comes up with a plan to help revive it, and his suggestion for a Test world championship is an intriguing idea deserving close study. It is the kind of innovative thinking Ian put into his captaincy and that is needed in the board rooms of the ICC and its member boards.

When Ian Chappell writes on cricket, he does so with the knowledge of someone who has been involved as Test player and captain, and as professional observer as television commentator. All who have followed his career would expect nothing less than a forthright, critical and sincere assessment of the game as he sees it. It is not his style to mask his feeling behind diplomatic language for fear of offending someone. He tells it like it is, and always has.

WHAT'S WRONG WITH TEST CRICKET?

"The ICC Will be Guilty of Murder..."

Two personal memories exemplify, for me, batting at International level. The first is of a 'Test' against the Rest of the World at the Gabba in the 1971-72 season. I vividly recall the first few overs I faced from Pakistan leg-spinner Intikhab Alam. He gave me a thorough examination, with each delivery in his repertoire pitched on a length as he constantly varied his pace and line.

The other occasion was a century I made against Clive Lloyd's West Indies pace attack in 1975-76 on a bouncy WACA pitch. It is most likely the nearest I'll ever come to being in a pitched battle, and apart from that experience and running with the bulls in Pamplona, I can only wonder how I might have fared fighting in a war.

The exhilaration of first surviving, and then blossoming, in contests like those is a batsman's reward for all the years of practice. It's on occasions like those that you realise a Test match is well named; it's a complete test of a player's skill, intelligence and courage.

At times, one could be forgiven for thinking the International Cricket Conference (ICC), the administrators who are appointed to protect the best interests of the game, are trying to reduce the level of those three requirements.

If Test cricket is killed off, it'll be an inside job; the ICC will be guilty of murder. Their method is to administer a slow poison in the form of lethal doses of lunatic legislation.

The best examples of this are the front-foot no-ball law, the experimental law for short-pitched bowling and their glacial reaction to slow over rates. These three laws are at the heart of the delicate balance between bat and ball, so vital to the survival of Test cricket, and yet the ICC either administer the wrong dosage to the ailing patient, or stand by and do nothing as breathing becomes more difficult.

At a time when there's a crying need for less draws and more activity in Test cricket, the administrators keep producing solutions which are more boring than the perceived problem. Even worse, in the case of their ruling on short-pitched deliveries, everyone from players to former players, from the public to the latest intake of youngsters at the cricket academy, thinks it's stupid.

In the case of that ruling, the ICC solution was the equivalent of loading Russ Hinze on the other end of a see-saw, because they believed it was originally being weighed down by Kerry Packer. Consequently the balance, which was ridiculously in favour of fast bowlers because of the slow over rates, has now been disproportionately shifted to favour the willow wielders, who face a maximum of one bouncer per batsmen, per over.

These anomalies occur in some cases because the administrators are out of touch with reality, and in other cases because they appear to be more concerned with looking after the interests of their own country than those of the game.

The front-foot no-ball and slow over rates are classic examples of what I'm talking about. Part of the reason for the slow over rates is the ridiculously high number of no-balls being delivered under the front-foot law.

The front-foot law must go. It was introduced in order to stop the excessive 'draggers' who appeared in the late fifties and early sixties. It achieved that aim, for which batsmen can be thankful, but now it's become a boring blight on the game.

Everytime a no-ball is delivered it's like four cars coming from different directions, all arriving at a roundabout at the same time, then screeching to a halt—the anticipation is high, but nothing happens. Against a pace bowler (and most attacks are loaded with quickies these days), the batsmen usually only have time to push the ball back along the pitch. The bowler then ambles over to the non-striker's end, places his foot where it cuts the crease, and has a lengthy discussion with the umpire about the increase in players' boot sizes in the last thirty years.

Meanwhile, the batsman is not only deprived of any realistic scoring chance, but is also made to wait an age for his next opportunity, while the bowler has regained his composure. During all this inactivity, the fans begin to search for a book or a beer.

Apart from bringing the game to a grinding halt, the law also hampers the umpires in adjudicating on decisions. If an umpire delays lifting his eyes until a fast bowler's front foot has landed, the ball is well on its way before he picks it up in flight, leaving precious little time to judge where it pitches or to detect a faint edge. If the umpire tries to cheat a bit and estimate where the fast bowler's foot will land, more no-balls result.

Most of the no-balls called for over-stepping are in the range of one to ten centimetres; in other words, nothing that is going to make a scrap of difference to the bowler's pace. I'll bet if you asked any batsman worth his place in a Test side if he'd rather have the umpire calling ten centimetre no-balls, or allow him more time to adjudicate on the decisions that relate to the batsman's survival, he'd opt for the latter.

Solution: a commonsense back-foot law which will significantly reduce the number of no-balls and will not allow draggers to creep back into the game. In conjunction with this law, demand that teams average a minimum of a hundred balls per hour each day, to be bowled within normal playing hours.

Effect: the reduced number of no-balls would make it easier for teams to maintain a decent over rate. There's also a good chance that the odd no-ball delivered would be slammed either to or over the boundary, providing extra entertainment for the crowd, while adequately punishing the bowler. I'm sure we'd also see an improvement in the standard of decision making, with the umpires having more time to follow the ball in flight.

There's an added advantage for a quick-thinking cricketer. I once saw Keith Miller, playing for NSW (under the back-foot no-ball law), chase a lofted shot at the Adelaide Oval. He deliberately let the ball fall through his hands, and the crowd jeered him unmercifully. However, they went strangely silent when he grabbed the ball on the first bounce, whirled around and threw to the bowler's end to gain a run out from a *no-ball.*

From what I can gather, most umpires and administrators who are against a back-foot no-ball law are worried about the re-emergence of draggers. Why? With a modicum of commonsense this can't happen. The umpire always has to watch the back foot land to see if the boot is cutting the return crease. Having seen where that lands, he then has a fair idea of whether the front foot is going to be close to the line, and if he needs confirmation, the umpire, as he lifts his eyes in the direction of the striker, can note where the front foot is on its way to earth.

Once the umpire has watched a couple of deliveries to establish where each bowler has to land his back foot to ensure he's bowling from the full distance, he then places a white disc to help both himself and the bowler know what's legitimate and what's not. This means the umpire can then forget about the front foot and, by concentrating solely on the back foot, come out with early no-ball calls. He'll soon know if a bowler starts dragging excessively and will be able to penalise him with an early no-ball call; meanwhile he has more time to adjudicate on the difficult decisions.

Under this system there will be, I grant you, a few times when the bowler will be a centimetre or two over the front line. That may be the undisclosed reason why a back-foot no-ball law isn't reintroduced. I think some administrators and umpires are worried about the scrutiny of the camera in those cases. I say, to hell with that, make the change because it helps everybody on the playing field and most importantly, it's in the best interests of the game. Under the present law, any bowler looking to intimidate a batsman is not going to be put off by the thought of conceding one run. That means nothing if it allows the bowler to send down a speeding missile that singes the batsman's eyebrows. Balance that one run against the psychological damage done to the batsman (especially if he's just arrived at the crease) and you can see it's not a penalty as far as the quickie is concerned.

What is a deterrent is the shattering scream of "NOOOOO...ball" in the bowler's ear just as he's about to release a thunderbolt. The end result is even more shattering if the delighted batsman whacks a four (or six) by taking advantage of the early call and enlisting, as John Arlott once described it, "a threateningly high backlift".

A back-foot law would reduce the number of no-balls and increase the thrills when one was delivered. It would also help improve over rates and that is of paramount importance to the game of cricket. First, there is the obvious reason. The more balls bowled, the more opportunities to take wickets and similarly to score runs, hence a better day's entertainment for everybody concerned. Then there's the important consideration of the balance between bat and ball.

The prime task for administrators when tampering with the laws is to maintain the status quo like evenly balanced scales. The fewer laws required to preserve this balance, the less opportunity for manipulation by captains and players.

During their career most captains are guilty of trying to slow the game down when they are in trouble. It's human nature, and umpires need to be given solid support by administrators to stop such shenanigans.

Since adopting a policy of consistently selecting four fast bowlers, however, the West Indies have incorporated slowing the over rates into their tactics. The worst example was at Trinidad in 1990, when Desmond Haynes thwarted England's attempt to go two up in the series, by slowing the over rate to around eight an hour.

The West Indies were by no means the first to adopt this policy. Len (later Sir Len) Hutton significantly reduced the number of deliveries the Australians received in a day's play in 1954-55 and, combined with the devastating speed of Frank 'Typhoon' Tyson, it proved to be a resounding success. It doesn't matter who is slowing the game down, it is a most unfair tactic and should be outlawed.

The administrators should demand that teams bowl at an average minimum rate of at least 100 balls per hour. They should also stipulate that the minimum number of overs must be completed within the prescribed playing hours, not at some time preceding midnight.

When approached on their lack of backbone in enforcing better over rates, most administrators say they've tried, but the players aren't responsive. In other words, fines haven't worked.

Not surprising, when the fines in the case of the West Indies in 1988-89 were refunded by the ACB. I would even hazard a guess that the money actually found it's way back into the pockets of the offending West Indies players, although the ACB has stressed that wasn't their intention in returning the money to the West Indies Board.

Scrap the fines. Punish the man responsible for the slow over rates. If an offending captain was suspended for two Test matches, there would be a huge scream from the camp that was penalised, but there would never be another infringement. Teams can bowl their overs much quicker if they are forced to and especially if they are made to realise that the administrators are *serious* about improving over rates. As a matter of interest, if they were *really* serious, surely they'd introduce legislation to make it compulsory for all grounds to have permanent sightscreens, like the Adelaide Oval, where no move has to be made when a bowler changes from over to around the wicket.

By drumming home the need to dramatically improve over rates, it would also make International cricketers realise that if they don't contribute something to an increase in the value for money, the fans won't attend. If Test match crowds dwindle, cricketers will soon be joining the ever increasing number of people out of work.

The players may complain that they are overworked now and this would only add to the load. That being the case, a good compromise would be a compulsory rest day during all Tests. This isn't such a bad idea anyway, because it would help players overcome slight injuries and the extra deterioration of the pitch would enhance the case for good spinners. It would also allow the administrators more flexibility in trying to recoup playing time in cases of rain. The recent protest by spectators at Edgbaston, who threw cushions onto the ground during the rain-marred first Test between England and Pakistan, is a sure sign that people are fed up to the back teeth with the lack of value for money received at Test matches.

This sort of tough legislation would ensure International captains quickly dropped all the time wasting habits that creep into the game. The sight of Viv Richards moving at the speed of a sun dial to chat with one of his bowlers during an over would mercifully be a thing of the past. You don't need to be endowed with a Richie Benaud cricket brain to realise the difference for the fielding side in the two following examples.

EXAMPLE A: The West Indies bowl seventy-six overs in five and a half hours play, with the four fast men each bowling seventeen and Viv and Carl Hooper splitting eight.

EXAMPLE B: The West Indies bowl ninety-two overs (that's five and a half hours at the rate of a hundred balls per hour), with the four quick men each bowling twenty-one and Viv and Carl again splitting eight.

The extra twenty-four balls for each fast bowler may not sound like it would have a huge impact, but it means there is less rest between balls. It also means the pace bowlers will be tiring in the final session and any batsmen good enough to hang around that long can extract revenge. This hasn't been the case in recent times, and consequently the delicate balance between bat and ball is unrealistically in favour of the fast bowlers in Example A. From the fans' point of view, there's almost one hundred extra balls in Example B for the batsmen to score off or, alternatively, the fielding side to claim wickets.

While fast bowlers are fresh they'll bang a few in short to see, firstly, if the pitch has much bounce, and secondly, if the batsman wants to be at the crease, or if he'd rather be lounging by the pool. That's accepted practice. In the early part of the day they're bowling to the top order batsmen who should expect their back-foot technique to be tested.

Later in the day when the fast bowlers are tiring, a good back-foot player will actually look forward to receiving a few short-pitched deliveries. To some batsmen these are a long hop to be scored from, while the more timid variety view them as a hand grenade about to explode in their face.

The ICC wouldn't have had to change the law on short-pitched bowling if they'd taken the following steps: (a) Made teams bowl a respectable number of deliveries in a day's play, (b) Produced a commonsense back-foot law, (c) Asked umpires to call any ball from which a batsman can't play a normal cricket shot a wide, and (d) Told umpires they'd receive strong support if they strictly enforced the law regarding intimidation.

By taking such measures they would also achieve the following objectives: a more even balance between bat and ball, without dictating how teams must be selected; a decline in the number of short-pitched deliveries; an improvement in umpiring standards; less friction between players and umpires; more results; and increased entertainment value.

To complete the transformation of Test cricket, there are a couple more things an active ICC could do.

Firstly, they should campaign to ensure that Test pitches, where possible, have reasonable and predictable bounce. Bounce is an important ingredient in the playing of good cricket. It allows batsmen to play a full range of shots and it assists good pace, swing and spin bowlers, because when they induce a mistake and gain an edge, the ball carries a good distance. A bouncy pitch is also harsh on medium-pace naggers, which adds to it's attraction. While they're at it, they should also encourage curators not to saturate the outfield prior to a Test and to cut the outfield grass low. A lush outfield which looks good on television has become the fashion, but it doesn't make for entertaining cricket. The ball retains it's shine too long and the batsmen aren't properly rewarded for their good shots.

Secondly, the ICC should meet with all International captains, umpires and Board chairmen to explain the vital need for good cricket, better over rates and a less antagonistic attitude towards umpires. During the discussions it should be made clear that Test cricket is in peril and needs a more aggressive outlook from everybody, starting with the executives and ranging all the way through to the players.

It should also be made abundantly clear that the umpires are in charge in the middle and that they will be backed to the hilt by the administrators. If players transgress, a few solid suspensions would ram home the message. Some of the things officials need to crack down on are excessive appealing, fieldsmen charging umpires when appealing, and batsmen trying to influence an umpire's decision by indicating whether the ball has hit the bat or the person.

I must say I was disappointed, but not surprised, that such a meeting wasn't held during the World Cup in 1992. Surely this would have been the perfect opportunity to get each country to do its bit to improve Test cricket. However, the ICC missed the chance, something they do regularly. In fact, if a wicket-keeper had their abysmal record, he'd be flat out getting a game with the Gulargambone fourth eleven.

However, I think that with the ICC's current lack of credibility, any such meeting would have had little, if any, effect. As I discuss in the chapter on the power of the veto, I believe it's time to scrap the ICC and put in place an internationally credible Board that runs the game on a truly global basis and with the best interests of the game as their top priority.

From the players' point of view, the law of Test cricket that really matters is their own. It says, "When you've got 'em, make the most of it, because when you haven't, you're going to cop it." This is a simple recognition of the power of pace bowling. The best examples of this law at work were the first two Ashes series in Australia in the seventies. In the 1970-71 battle England, headed by John Snow, had the pace advantage and the Australian batsmen were made to hop. In the return bout in 1974-75, it was Australia with Lillee and Thomson who called the tune.

In his book *Swanton in Australia*, the outspoken English cricket writer E.W. 'Jim' Swanton expressed the opinion that the short-pitched stuff was overdone in both series and that the respective captains, Ray Illingworth and myself, should have better controlled the bowlers.

I'm sure Ray felt as I did, that this was a matter entirely for the umpires to decide. I can assure Swanton that as a captain you don't spend a lot of time counting the number of bouncers your fast bowlers send down and certainly, when one has an opposing batsman dangling on the end of the line, there's no way you're going to suggest he cut the cord.

As a matter of interest, my view of the short-pitched battle that was supposedly raging on the field in 1974-75 was this.

For starters, I had first-hand knowledge that the English press were not convinced Dennis Lillee could recover from his bad back and bowl fast again. They also thought that news of Jeff Thomson's extreme pace was just another example of the Australian propaganda machine at work. I became aware of this while I was in England in 1974 doing some work with Trans Australia Airlines (TAA). As part of my duties, I held a press conference at Headingley, during the Pakistan v. England first Test, and the journalists asked me questions on both those matters. On hearing my answers, they proceeded to decry my opinions.

It would appear that this impression then permeated the English camp, because their fast bowlers, Bob Willis and Peter Lever in particular, came out bouncing when Australia batted first in the opening Test of the 1974-75 series. It was during that match at the Gabba that Dennis Lillee, who had been bounced out by Tony Greig, uttered the prophetic words on returning to the dressingroom: "Just remember who started this; they did. But we'll bloody finish it."

And finish it he did.

Notice I said 'he' not 'they'. Every time Jeff Thomson bowled a bouncer in that series it went way over the batsman's head and often over wicket-keeper Rodney Marsh's head. The only time it ever served any value was in a couple of incidents in

Perth when, after passing over Rodney's head, the ball crashed into the fence on the half-volley. That had a certain value on the Thomson intimidation scale.

But Thommo's really dangerous deliveries were the ones that rose sharply from just short of a good length and went for the throat like a Doberman under orders. That is just plain good bowling and, along with his extreme pace, it was the reason Thommo was, for two and half seasons until he damaged his shoulder, the most lethal bowler I've seen.

There is no way a captain is going to order his bowler to stop bowling well. And, until 1 October, 1991, a good delivery wasn't illegal according to the laws of cricket. Consequently the umpires didn't intervene while Jeff's thunderbolts were terrorising the English batsmen.

I was spoken to once about short-pitched bowling during the 1974-75 series, by umpire Tom Brooks in Perth. Tom told me that Brian Luckhurst, who was batting in the second innings with a broken finger, was not to receive any bouncers. On that occasion I told Tom I disagreed with him and gave him my reasons. But when he re-asserted his position, I said that he was in charge of the game and if that's what he wanted, that's what he'd get.

The only other time I was spoken to was by Robin Bailhache at the MCG during the third Test. Robin said that Alan Knott had complained about Dennis swearing at him, and asked me to sort it out. This was done immediately and there was no recurrence in the series. Years later I asked Alan about the incident. He had no recollection of it and said he doubted he would have complained. Which probably means it was a thoughtful piece of umpiring by Robin.

Throughout that series I had the feeling that Dennis was bowling like a man who believed every ball might be his last. He had just spent twelve months out of the game on a strenuous rebuilding programme after suffering bad back problems, so this was understandable. I still didn't feel that at any time Dennis overdid the short stuff, but there was no doubting his desire to, as he said, "Finish *it*."

Only once did I feel sickened by a bouncer in that series. Dennis bowled one at Geoff Arnold with the second new ball as we tried to wrap up the Ashes on the last day at the SCG. The ball passed about two inches over Geoff's head (no helmets in those days), as he turned his back on the ball. We all let out a huge sigh of relief in the slips when the ball thudded into Rodney's gloves, and I wouldn't mind betting Dennis was pleased to hear that noise as well.

But no captain could have stopped that. A bowler has a mind of his own and believe me, captains can't read 'em, even if they would dearly love to. I believe the matter of short-pitched bowling must be left entirely in the hands of the umpires.

I should also point out my view, as a batsman, of short-pitched bowling, which is further evidence of why it must be left up to the umpire. Batting at number three, I expected that on occasions I would receive three bouncers in an eight ball over. But in all my years of playing Test cricket I didn't ever feel that I was bombarded to the point of excess.

In 1974-75 some of the press seemed to be a little uneasy over Dennis Lillee's assertion on television (also written earlier in a book) that he aimed "to hit the batsman somewhere between the stomach and the rib cage".

I didn't see what all the fuss was about. Lillee had to have a target, he can aim wherever he likes, because as far as I'm concerned, the batsman has a bat in his hand. For Lillee to hit his target the batsman has to miss the ball. If a top order batsman misses one aimed in that area on a normal Test match pitch, he's either taken his eye off the ball, or he needs to pay a visit to OPSM. I'll bet if all fast bowlers were as honest as Dennis they'd tell you they're aiming at some part of the batsman's anatomy when they deliver a short-pitched ball.

If, however, a fast bowler is aiming to intimidate or injure a tailender, then that is a different proposition. Under the previous law on short-pitched bowling there was ample opportunity for umpires to protect a player they thought was being intimidated. However, problems arose because of the lack of communication between the administrators and the umpires. I'm sure the men in black and white felt they weren't getting the support they needed to enforce the law. Consequently, we encountered ludicrous situations.

One umpire in England warned Merv Hughes, "That's enough," when he bowled two short ones in an over to Robin Smith. Now Smith doesn't need too much help—he can kill a fielder at twenty paces with one of his thunderous cut shots. However, when Pakistan tailender Tauseef Ahmed courageously withstood a bombarding from the same bowler at the MCG, the umpires didn't say a word. Hell, if that wasn't intimidation, bordering on bullying, then Rambo's a pacifist.

I have always believed that any weakness of character in a batsman is as legitimate a target as a weakness outside off stump. The bouncer is an important part of the game. However, problems arise when it's the tailenders who are being tested, not the batsmen.

To a large degree this has come about because of the protective equipment that is now available to players, and the change in attitude this has encouraged among tailend batsmen. Protected by more armoury than a medieval knight, a tailender can feel impregnable when facing a fast bowler. Consequently, he's more likely to get in behind every delivery and defend for all he's worth, which is frustrating for a pace bowler and, might I add, the people watching the game.

There is nothing more boring in the game of cricket than a tailender unable to score and a fast bowler unable to dismiss him because he's just good enough to stop the balls on the stumps. The game comes to a shuddering halt.

It's often at this point when a fast bowler tries to relieve his frustration by pounding the ball in short in an attempt to have the tailender capitulate. Adding to the increasing instances of this occurring is the lack of quality spin bowling around, which means that captains aren't turning to spinners to bring about the demise of a slogging tailender.

Compare that with a time when tailenders weren't padded and had in mind only that they might smote one from an opposing paceman into an adjacent field. This may have brought the odd warning shot from a fast bowler (a bouncer aimed slightly wide of the tailender), but in general the quickie was prepared to back his ability to bowl out a slogging tailender.

I'm sure it was the sight of fast bowlers bombarding tailenders with short-pitched stuff which brought about the introduction of the experimental law. Unfortunately, the drafting of this new law on short-pitched bowling came about because the administrators only looked at the most obvious problem and didn't think the whole matter through.

The administrators over-reacted when announcing that from 1 October, 1991, only one bouncer per batsman per over is permitted in Test cricket. They then compounded their mistake by defining a fast short-pitched ball as one "which passes, or would have passed, above the shoulder of a batsman standing upright at the crease". In the case of a bowler transgressing, he'll be no-balled on the first two occasions (the second time he'll be told it's a final warning) and the third time he's out of the attack forthwith and for the rest of the innings.

To underline the stupidity of this definition, in some parts of the cricket world you can now bowl a short-pitched delivery that is a no-ball in a Test match, but legitimate in a Limited-overs game. With logic like that, is it any wonder Americans have trouble understanding cricket?

However, this legislation goes even further by outlawing good deliveries and it could also mean that the hook shot will become as rare as sightings of the Tasmanian Tiger. But the real showstopper is its potential for creating a ding-dong argument between the fielding side and a poor unfortunate umpire who correctly uses the law to reprieve a batsman caught off a bouncer that is deemed a no-ball.

Consider also the added burden on the umpires who have to keep track of which batsman has received a bouncer and which one hasn't during each over. If you have a couple of players who continually rotate the strike and there's a loss of wicket in the over, then this task becomes a nightmare, as well as being a further distraction from the main duty of the umpire—judging whether a batsman is out or not out.

Following the legislation, there were defensive murmurings from the ICC that under the new experimental law, bowlers were still able to deliver in excess of one hundred bouncers in a day's play. That is not the point. Under the new law the batsman is given too much warning about the bowler's upcoming strategy, by knowing he's only going to receive one bouncer per over. That's unfair.

The ICC say they want self-regulation of the bouncer. Well, they could have achieved that with the measures I mentioned earlier, without taking anything away from the bowler's armoury.

Instead, the administrators have produced a piece of legislation which, apart from its nonsensical qualities, is totally in favour of batsmen. The most damaging aspect of a bouncer is not necessarily the delivery itself, but the uncertainty its presence creates in a batsman's mind. If he's unsure whether the bouncer is going to be "this one, the next one or the one after", it can derail his train of thought and leave him vulnerable to an assortment of other deliveries. There are also times when a good bouncer has a batsman in trouble and needs to be followed by a similar delivery. Under the present law that can't happen legally.

As an example of the uncertainty the short-pitched ball places in a batsman's mind, take England's Graeme Hick. One of the reasons he's currently a struggling Test player after amassing a boat load of runs at county level, is the threat of the bouncer. Cricket needs to distinguish between the genuine Test player and a good first-class player, and Hick should have the chance to assert himself against pace bowling, without help from a law.

When one Australian Cricket Board member was trying to drum up support in the 1980s to eradicate the bouncer, I wrote that it would diminish Test cricket to the point of being nothing more than a batting exhibition. If the reason for doing it was to reduce the effectiveness of the West Indies, I added that it would fail (they had a strong batting line-up at the time) because every now and again they would win a game by "scoring 1200 to the opposition's 1100".

To eradicate the bouncer makes as much sense as talk of allowing only one serve in tennis. This recent piece of legislation by the ICC is not as bad as that, but it could be a seven-league leap in that direction.

With good commonsense legislation, Test cricket can attract reasonable crowds and provide the players with the searching test they need to keep their skills honed for other versions of the game.

Whilst Test cricket can't survive on its own, equally, Limited-overs cricket would be doomed in isolation. Without the skills provided by a wide variety of players with different styles, which can only be acquired over time and proper testing, a steady diet of Limited-overs cricket, with its inherent constraints and similarity of procedure, would result in eventual boredom for both the players and the spectators. The very name of the game tells you it couldn't survive on its own, because it's *limited*.

Test cricket is the players' game—the ultimate test. Limited-overs cricket is the fans' game—the best in entertainment. Together they make a fine couple; parted they would be as sad as a broken marriage.

One-day cricket's strength, its ability to provide a result the same day, is also its greatest liability. Its limitations deprive bowlers of putting in a lionhearted performance, it makes a team's recovery from early disasters highly unlikely and leaves only the top order batsmen with the option of building an innings into something of brilliance.

Apart from the actual limit of the number of overs in an innings, all the other constraints in Limited-overs cricket are placed on the bowlers. I think that is unfair. I don't agree that these matches have to be high-scoring affairs or that a bit of variety in pitches is bad. I think Limited-overs cricket should be a contest, hard fought and hopefully close, but not stage-managed by reducing the bowler's part to nothing more than that of a self-propelled ball machine.

I also like a bit of bounce in a One-day pitch. It allows the batsman the opportunity of playing some horizontal bat shots, especially if they adopt universally the law that only the ball passing above the batsman's head is an illegal delivery. As I've already mentioned, the playing condition in Australia, where a ball passing over shoulder height when a batsman takes his normal stance is deemed a no-ball, is ridiculous.

Once again it creates enormous difficulties for the umpires, while not allowing the bowlers any margin for error with a short delivery. But worst of all, it does the thinking for an enraged fast bowler.

If, in the final over with the match in the balance, a fast bowler wants to go berserk and bounce a batsman, why should the law help him? If he's so angry that he puts retribution ahead of his team's chances of victory, let him go ahead. The selectors will punish him much better than any law. A bouncer in that situation is the worst ball a bowler could deliver. It allows the batsman the luxury of using the 360 degrees of the field, as against a yorker on the stumps, which restricts him to about sixty degrees.

With just a minimum of fine tuning, Test and One-day cricket can complement each other perfectly. This is exactly the way it should be, as there's a marvellous give and take quality about the two. Consider things like the skill and athleticism that One-day cricket has brought to the allround standard of fielding in the longer version of the game. Or the marvellous attacking skills of a Viv Richards or a Wasim Akram honed in Test cricket, which flourish equally in the more rushed routing of an opponent.

Test cricket is currently ailing because the ICC is so immersed in political manoeuvring, that it is totally incapable of having as its main objective "to above all, administrate in the best interests of the game".

I was chatting with the current ICC chairman Sir Colin Cowdrey at the Auckland airport the morning after the magnificent World Cup semi-final between Pakistan and New Zealand. In the middle of a mixture of nattering and some chattering about the cricket, a Pakistan journalist excused himself and posed the question (to Colin), "Has anyone ever thought about a World Cup of Test cricket yet?"

Colin said, "No, I don't think so."

On hearing that I said, "Actually, I wrote a piece on that very subject for the Melbourne *Age* just over twelve months ago." I then went on to briefly outline my plan, which was based on the Rugby League World Cup qualifying system. It's quite feasible, and reaching a stage of two teams left in the competition is nowhere near as long-winded and cumbersome as one might imagine.

My idea was to have a final that was 'a duel to the death', with the winner every four years being crowned the World Champion. This would slot into the middle of the World Cup four-year span. Not only would a competition like this be a showpiece for the longer game, it could help add spice to regular Test series, with captains trying to juggle their World Championship needs with those of the series in progress.

The journalist from Pakistan was interested in my ideas, as he'd been trying to create some interest on the subject himself. Colin's response was only, "You should get one of your delegates to propose that to the ICC."

It was interesting to contrast Colin's approach to that of West Indies cricket commentator, writer and allround enthusiast for the game, Tony Cozier. On hearing of the idea, he immediately asked me to send him a copy of my article so he could reproduce it in one of his Caribbean cricket magazines, with a view to fanning the flames of discussion.

It's Coze's enthusiasm and urgency which is missing from cricket administration when it comes to important issues. I sometimes wonder if they realise the need for urgency when it comes to Test cricket. The patient is ailing, there's no time for the doctors to discuss who should operate, it's time to make an accurate incision.

THE VETO, RACISM AND A BETTER UNDERSTANDING

"Permanently Discredited and Abandoned."

In his thought-provoking classic 'War', Jamaican Reggae master Bob Marley sang about the need to "permanently discredit and abandon the philosophy" that any one race is superior and any other is inferior.

The song was written about the game of life. It applies equally to the game of cricket.

The fact that England and Australia, as two of the three founding nations (South Africa was the other) of the International Cricket Conference (ICC) still have the power of veto over the other full members, is, as you would expect, a source of great annoyance. It is a hangover from the days of the Imperial Cricket Conference which was founded in 1909. Some of the thinking of the aforementioned administrators is in tune with that era.

Even if they don't listen to Marley's music, those officials could at least heed the words. There have been many times when I have felt the ICC should be 'permanently discredited and abandoned' for either sitting on the fence or, when they have moved, falling into a vat of foolishness before they acted.

In 1991, when I said on a television programme in Kingston, Jamaica, that "for England and Australia to maintain the power of veto at the ICC is an insult to the other full members," there was loud applause from the studio audience. The reaction would have been appreciated down the road at the local Melbourne CC; it's just a pity it didn't carry as far as Melbourne in Australia and to the Long Room at Lord's.

I'm sure that the power of veto is at the root of all the plotting and politicking that goes on at the ICC. The tardy and aimless administration that has trickled forth from that body under the guise of law-making since I've been involved in the game should be a punishable offence. It is the cricketing equivalent of criminal neglect, especially as it comes at a time when a bit of prompt, commonsense action would have been of great benefit to the ailing game of Test cricket.

Meanwhile, we get a continuous stream of weeping and wailing from England and some quarters in Australia, saying in between sobs, "Kerry Packer has put the skids under Test cricket." Rubbish. As I've already stated, if Test cricket is allowed to die, it'll be an inside job.

I played at the tailend of the era when some Indian and Pakistani players were subservient. I will never forget the look on Rodney Marsh's face when he joined me in the middle of the SCG with Australia deep in trouble at 5/70 against Pakistan in 1972-73. Rod had just passed substitute fielder Majid Usman, a budding young fast bowler, and he thought the Pakistani was taking the mickey when he exclaimed, "Oh mister Marsh, I am 'oping you hit de ball wery, wery hard today and make many, many runs."

The reason for the strangulated look on Rodney's face was the sudden realisation that the young man sincerely meant every word he'd spoken. Rod Marsh was his hero.

The advent of competitors like Imran Khan, Sarfraz Nawaz and Javed Miandad has changed all that for Pakistan. I have found all three to be excellent company off the field, but during playing hours they will give as good as they get, which is exactly the way it should be. Hence Pakistan's rise to a position of power in international cricket in the last fifteen years.

There appears to be some resentment of this in world cricket, especially from England and Australia. You get the distinct impression that Pakistan were much more popular when they were easily pushed around.

I have made it abundantly clear that the odd word between

players on the field has never bothered me. I was taught that "sticks and stones will break your bones, but words will never hurt you".

Australia has always been a forceful and aggressive cricketing nation. The great allrounder of the last century, George Giffen, wrote about Frederick 'The Demon' Spofforth, "I verily believe he has frightened more batsmen out than many bowlers have fairly and squarely beaten."

The same words could well have applied to Dennis 'The Menace' Lillee from 1971 to 1984. The methods may have varied a little over the years, but there was never any doubt about the competitiveness.

I don't think Australian cricketers are in any position to start admonishing Pakistan players who have a few words to them on the field. This happened in the World Cup match in Perth in 1992. I have no problem if a player 'returns the compliment', but the departing batsman must continue heading in the direction of the dressingroom, not return to the crease to wag a finger as was the case at the WACA. I believe much of this lack of tolerance occurs because teams don't spend enough time mixing after play. The custom of having a drink with the opposition in the dressingroom following a day's play must be retained and importantly, it should be done at all times, not just with those teams you like.

It's not hard to understand this courtesy diminishing, as some of the cricket is played at night and finishes late. Also, there's so much cricket played that familiarity can breed contempt. But I think more effort should be made to maintain some contact between competing teams.

There are many good reasons for this custom. Most importantly it is common courtesy, but it also helps to get to know and understand the opposition better. This can be of great benefit on the field.

In 1970-71 I noticed Rod Marsh spending a lot of time talking to Geoff Boycott at the end of each day's play. At first I marked this down as shrewdness on Rodney's part, as each team only received a dozen (large) bottles of beer. I figured

Rodney had chosen a non-drinker to talk with so he didn't have to share his bottle.

However, on further enquiry I discovered Rodney was onto a gold mine. As he explained, he was talking to Boycott after play one day and mentioned how well another England player was batting. "Aye, he is," replied Geoffrey, "but yoor bowlin't wruung line to 'im."

Never one to miss an opportunity, Rodney piped up, "And what line should we be bowling?"

Whereupon Geoffrey gave him a rundown on his teammate's batting. Thereafter, Rodney sought out Boycott regularly and tossed in a different English player's name. It proved to be a worthwhile exercise.

Apart from finding out valuable information, the dressingroom is the place where any disputes that occur on the field can be watered down. If harsh words have been spoken on the field, it's amazing how it can be joked about later, even by the protagonists, when they're amongst teammates in the more relaxed atmosphere of the dressingroom.

And it doesn't have to be in the dressingroom. During a WSC match in Mildura I'd become extremely frustrated as the World XI made a great recovery, thanks to some aggressive batting by Imran Khan and Alan Knott. We eventually clinched victory by just a few runs when Imran was out for 98.

I was still hot under the collar over dropped catches, and as Imran walked past me I made some mindless comment that it was "about time your bloody arse ran out". A couple of hours later, I turned up at the dining room of the motel where the teams were staying to find the restaurant full. As I stood there waiting for a table, South African Eddie Barlow got up and paid his bill, leaving one empty seat in the room.

Without any hesitation I walked over and sat down. Right next to Imran. As if on cue, the other World XI players got up and left the table to pay their bill, leaving Imran with a half eaten fish meal and me as his sole dinner companion.

I said, "Good evening Imran. Great knock of yours today."

He looked at me amazed. "Thank you Ian," he replied, "but

I didn't expect you to be talking to me."

"Why not?" I asked, a little surprised.

"In Pakistan," Imran explained, "if two players exchange words on the field, that's it. They don't talk again."

I laughed and said, "It's different in Australia, that's accepted as part of the game. Afterwards," I added, "it's all forgotten."

With that sorted out we had a friendly chat over dinner, but on the field continued to have a very competitive outlook. We have remained friends ever since.

I don't understand players who say that you can't sit down and have a drink or a meal with an opponent and still remain the fiercest of enemies on the field. Australian players do it all the time when they are competing against their mates in Sheffield Shield cricket.

I was staggered to read of Dean Jones' attitude in an interview for Jack Egan's book, *Extra Cover*. While discussing the West Indies' fast bowlers, Jones says, "Why should you be going hammer and tongs out in the middle and all of a sudden become best mates after the day's play?"

Then he really confused me with, "They talk about us not having a beer with them but it's a bit hard, to come up to them after the game and say well bowled. I enjoyed that one in the stomach. Or the broken finger."

In Dean's defence he made those comments after some early exchanges with the West Indies pace attack. He may well feel differently now.

I started going into the opposition dressingroom because I'd been taught it was the right thing to do. And I liked to unwind slowly after a day's play. But I quickly discovered it was also a good psychological ploy, especially if you'd taken a hammering. Who do you respect more as opponents? The team that slinks away with its tail between its legs after a defeat or a bad day, or a team that comes bustling into your room to say well played?

In my book, the slinkers are in trouble. I always felt we had them right where we wanted them—on the ropes. You knew the stayers were going to be back for more and you also knew they would be coming back hard. I was wary of those teams and they won my respect pretty quickly.

I think respect, or lack of it, is the main reason for the deterioration in the relationship between the West Indies and the Australian teams in recent times.

In Kim Hughes' period of captaincy, the Australian team complained that the West Indies weren't showing them enough respect. I'd respond to that by saying, "The Australians didn't earn it." Ever since that period there's been a distance between the two teams. That's sad when you know what it used to be like, even in times when the fast bowling was equally ferocious.

One of the great moments in my cricketing career occurred during the World Series Cricket tour of 1979, in the Queen's Park Oval dressingroom at Port of Spain, Trinidad. The tough WSC Australian opening batsman Bruce 'Stumpy' Laird made an exceptional hundred after the team had slumped to 5/32. Most of the players from both teams had been socialising in the West Indies' room, and I was just getting ready to shower when Rodney Marsh walked up to me with a glazed look in his eyes.

"Stumpy's just received the best compliment I've ever heard," said the emotional 'keeper. "Roy Fredericks (the WSC West Indies opener) just told him, 'I wish I'd made that hundred Stumpy.'"

For a moment I thought Rodney was going to shed a tear. I think he came close.

At the end of that series both teams spent a long time together in the dressingroom saying their farewells after an arduous and, at times, trying tour. It was handshakes all round. As we went back into our own room to pack, Rodney Marsh said to me, "That was a good feeling."

I looked up and said, "Yeah. And the best part is we won their respect, by taking everything they threw at us and coming back for more."

I have no doubt that the fact both teams had been involved in World Series Cricket helped. There is a bond between all those players who had the guts (as well as the financial foresight) to put their hands up and be counted. It will remain forever and I have no hesitation in saying it is one of the best things I gained from sixteen years of International cricket.

However, I also like to think that we won the West Indies' respect by our behaviour on the field. That's why I was disturbed to read Viv Richards' comments about Australian players telling him to, "F... off, you black bastard," in his book, *Hitting Across The Line.*

As far back as 1972-73, on the eve of the series against Pakistan in Australia and just a few weeks before we departed for the Caribbean, I called our players together. I told them that I would not stand for anyone prefixing their comments to an opposition player with the word "black". Apart from the common decency involved, I pointed out that they didn't, for example, say to an English player, "You lucky white bastard."

Following that meeting I was walking to the nets at the Adelaide Oval, when selector Sam Loxton dragged me aside. He started to explain that he didn't want any trouble between the two teams, especially on the score of racist remarks. I told Sam about the meeting that had just concluded and assured him there would be no trouble.

There wasn't. And neither was there any trouble in the Caribbean. In my period of captaincy, no Australian player made a derogatory reference about an opponent's colour in my hearing and I never had a complaint on it from an opposition captain. That's why I was disturbed to read Viv's reference.

I did two things. First, I asked Greg, who was captain of Australia in 1975-76 when Viv says the comments were made, if he'd heard anything. He said "No," and added, "there would have been trouble if I had." Not surprisingly, as we were brought up by the same parents.

Then, when Viv came to Australia to promote his book, I asked him about the reference during the vital West Indies/ Australia World Cup fixture at the MCG.

Viv named an Australian fast bowler as making the comments and said, "It only happened a couple of times." Then he chuckled, "I thought he was ignorant and I found out later he thought I was arrogant. We discovered this over a few drinks in England. Now we're mates."

One thing that has added to the likelihood of bad blood between players is the increase in the number of people who are involved in the running of cricket teams. Often former players are employed in these positions, and past grudges are dredged up, which in turn can lead to a gulf developing between the teams.

A captain is unlikely to say anything derogatory about the opposition because he knows he has to face them on the field the next day. The last thing you want to do is annoy an opposition batsman or fast bowler and give them a reason to vent their anger. However, a coach, a manager, or any hanger-on who feels empowered to unleash a comment, doesn't feel constrained by having to face the music the next day. These are the ones most likely to make an inflammatory statement and this usually leads to a response from the other side, which eventually spills over onto the field.

The less people making statements, especially in the heat of the moment, the less chance of ill-feeling.

The deterioration in Australia/West Indies relations is disappointing because the teams have so much in common, not only in their cricket history, but also in the way they play the game. Commonsense must prevail and bring about a return to normal relations. The ascendancy of Richie Richardson to the captaincy will help matters, and hopefully the Australian players will grasp this opportunity to heal the rift.

The Australian team don't have any trouble when they're playing England, but recent history shows a disturbing undercurrent in series with the West Indies and Pakistan.

The problem with Pakistan is one of distrust. It flared in Karachi in 1988, when Allan Border threatened to quit the tour halfway through the first Test.

This followed accusations by the management team of Colin Egar and Bob Simpson, of "incompetent umpiring and tampering with the pitch". That was the way Mike Coward, who was in Karachi at the time, described the situation in the *Sydney Morning Herald.*

In his book *Cricket Beyond The Bazaar*, Coward makes it quite clear the fracas in Pakistan was administration inspired. This is a classic case of how statements from management can affect the thinking and resultant actions of the players. Apart from being an excellent observer of the game and its personalities, Mike Coward's writing has always displayed the courage of his convictions, tinged with thoughtfulness.

In the late eighties he made an interesting observation when he said, "Ian, cricket's administrators in England and Australia are unable or unwilling to grasp the fact that the game has changed irrevocably. On the field, it is the West Indies who have challenged traditional attitudes and methods and boldly set new standards of professionalism." Warming to the subject he added, "Off the field Australia has broken new ground in programming, marketing, promotions and merchandising, yet still sees the cricket world as it was and not as it is. Like England, it remains suspicious of the power of the now dominant and persuasive Third World countries." Not so surprising then, although no more acceptable, is the attitude of the Australian team on the most recent tours of Pakistan and the West Indies. As a workmate of mine often reminds me, "The fish stinks from the head." As long as the administration continues to reek, the players will smell it.

In the Test series with Sri Lanka in the 1989-90 season, the Australians indulged in some old-fashioned school bullying, which should have been punished. The bowler concerned was Greg Campbell. Twice that I saw, he 'moved off his line' in his follow through and either made contact, or attempted to make contact, with his shoulder as the batsman was running.

That is the sort of action that is likely to provoke physical retaliation, which can lead to the game getting out of hand. In fact, a short while after Campbell had tried to 'bully' Aravinda De Silva, the larger and extremely competitive Rumesh Ratnayake took matters into his own hands and 'barrelled' the Tasmanian bowler while he was completing a run.

Apart from the fact that the umpires should have acted in the first place, why didn't the administrators bring about some justice in the matter? Campbell's performance was at least as bad as Dennis Lillee's involvement in the infamous incident with Javed at the WACA, for which Dennis was suspended.

It is also human nature to ask, "What would have happened if this incident had occurred against England or the West Indies?" The reply may well be another question. "Would the bowler have done the same thing to Robin Smith or Viv Richards?" Answer. I think not.

Is it any wonder then, that intelligent players and thinkers on the game like Sunil Gavaskar and Imran Khan are outspoken about aspects of the Australian game.

It is not whingeing, nor is it an over-reaction from someone who is racially insecure, when Sunil makes the observation, "When it's a mistake by a white umpire it's unfortunate human error, but the same benefit of the doubt is not given to umpires from the Third World. They are not only branded incompetent, but cheats as well."

And is it any wonder that Imran is a little bemused by the Australian sense of fair play. One Melbourne based writer who was in Karachi in 1988 lambasted the Pakistan team hierarchy in 1989-90, after they lost the first Test at the MCG.

This bloke, who must have been in an extreme state of confusion at the time of writing, castigated manager Intikhab Alam for not coming out and saying publicly what he thought. This followed Inty's statement that, "Any complaints we have about the umpiring will be aired in the appropriate place, the official report."

As two of the six second innings lbws given against Pakistan were 'shockers' in my opinion, I would have thought Intikhab deserved praise for setting a standard in diplomacy that the Australian team management didn't come close to in Pakistan.

It's easy to understand why Sunil and Imran are sceptical about criticism of umpires from the subcontinent. It's also easy to see why there is distrust among the administrative ranks, but it's damned difficult to understand why these problems aren't attended to, especially when people of intelligence and integrity are making the accusations.

The blow-up between Mike Gatting and Shakoor Rana in Pakistan in 1987, when the England captain and the Pakistani umpire had a heated discussion between balls, is a classic example of how a running battle between administrators spills over onto the field.

On that occasion, the England and Pakistani officials had been at loggerheads over umpire David Constant. This dispute had commenced in 1982 and then childishly escalated until neither side was prepared to give in. The officials should have used some commonsense and said, "Let's bury the hatchet on this matter." Instead, the series commenced in Pakistan with feelings at flashpoint.

And guess who paid the ultimate price? A player, of course. Mike Gatting may have been shafted at a later date over the Nottinghamshire barmaid affair, but that was only a cover-up, as he was always in trouble as England captain, following his on-field argument with umpire Shakoor Rana.

In most cases it's going to be the captain who has a disagreement with an umpire, because the captain is the only one allowed to discuss or argue a point of law. The Gatting case was just another example of how a mess caused by the officials was supposedly 'cleaned up' by punishing a player.

I'm sure this running battle between the officials of England and Pakistan can be traced back to the more aggressive approach of both the Pakistan players and administrators.

Imran hints at this in his book, *All Round View*. He says of Haseeb Ahsan, the manager in England in 1982, "He is not someone to take things lying down. Nor was he the kind of subservient Kala sahib or anglophile manager from the sub-continent that the English cricket administration were used to dealing with, and they were somewhat surprised by his combativeness."

Once again, there's that underlying suspicion that India and Pakistan were better liked when they did as they were told.

While England and Australia retain the power of veto at the ICC, distrust will remain and, not surprisingly, you won't be able to convince anybody from the Caribbean that colonialism isn't alive and well. It certainly doesn't make for better understanding among the cricket powers.

Ironically and tragically, as I wrote this chapter the Los Angeles race riots raged out of control. The unbelievable jury decision which acquitted four police officers in the Rodney King case has proved to be the catalyst for an unleashing of stored-up distrust, hatred and a feeling of hopelessness among the underprivileged people in America.

I've noticed in the reporting of these riots a new terminology entering the language. It is the description of black people as 'African Americans'. In a reference to slavery, one commentator on race relations went as far as saying, "This problem goes back over three hundred years. And," he concluded, "it won't be solved in a hurry."

Bob Marley also sang about the 'Buffalo Soldier' and how he was "stolen from Africa and brought to America". Marley goes on to explain how he was "fighting on arrival and fighting for survival". Tragically his fight still goes on, even though we are supposedly better educated and are certainly much better informed. Unfortunately, unless there's better understanding world wide, Marley's wish that "the basic human rights are equally guaranteed to all, without regard to race" will be a long time coming.

This is where sport, which has so often shone the torch to light the way in the past, can once again flick the switch. While cricket cannot correct the mistake made in America, it can at least ensure it doesn't commit the same error of failing to heed the many warning cries.

So far, the cries haven't been heard by the present administration. What the game needs is a body that rules on a global basis, with not just an international 'look', but with true international feeling.

When there are men who think deeply and care about the game like the recently retired Clive Lloyd and Sunil Gavaskar and the 'probably retired' Imran Khan; when you have such gentlemen, with the humour and firm opinions of Sir Garfield Sobers and Intikhab Alam, who have an understanding of the game and the need for aggressive, well-balanced cricket, nurtured in a more tolerant era, it shouldn't be difficult to put together a Board which could watch over the game with commonsense and dignity.

I don't think for one moment that only former players should be running the game. It takes a growing number of varied qualities to administer sport, especially on an international basis, and there are many other names with different areas of expertise that could be thrown into the ring. However, no list would be complete unless it contained the name Richie Benaud. An international thinking Board, with Richie at the helm, would have the respect and credibility necessary to bind the cricket world and make a concerted push to address the matters that are hampering the game at the moment.

At the July 1992 meeting of the ICC, Australia and England agreed in principle to relinquish their power of veto. Why do they always pussyfoot around at ICC meetings? Why agree in principle? Abolish the damn stupid power of veto and then get on with the business of being a responsible and international ruling body of the game of cricket, for heaven's sake.

Cricket needs to be run on a global basis by a body which has the overriding aim of serving the best interests of the game, rather than the playing of petty politics.

THE BEGINNINGS OF WORLD SERIES CRICKET

"Bradman's Attitude Contributed."

World Series Cricket, the three little words that 'traditional' cricket administrators never confused with 'I love you', the 'Three Little Words' in the song.

When it became obvious that World Series Cricket (WSC) would actually make it to the playing field, one high-ranking Australian Cricket Board (ACB) official said, "The Board has been stabbed in the back by the players."

To which I reply, "Bollocks."

On at least three occasions in the early seventies I was approached by sports entrepreneurs wanting to start up a professional cricket troupe. On each occasion I listened to the proposals and responded with, "You'll have to contact the Board, or Boards concerned, as they control the grounds."

On each occasion I was told later by the respective groups that they'd got nowhere with the Boards. This was despite assurances to the Boards that they didn't want to cut across Test cricket, only augment it. I wasn't surprised by the administrators' short-sighted view, as I had had an insight into their attitude to player payments on a number of previous occasions.

By 1974-75, dissatisfaction among Australian players over payments and conditions had been growing steadily for a few years. From my point of view, it all started on the 1969-70 tour of India and South Africa.

It was originally mooted as a joint tour of India and Pakistan.

However, the ACB couldn't reach a satisfactory financial arrangement with the Pakistan officials, so that leg was cancelled. Immediately, the South African Board put forward a proposal which was accepted by the ACB.

The arrangement was to play four Tests in South Africa at the conclusion of the Indian tour. This may have been financially sound, but it made no cricketing sense at all. Proceeding from India straight on to Pakistan isn't so bad, because playing conditions are similar and not much adjustment is required of the players. But three months in India on pitches that were slow and played low and assisted spinners, wasn't the ideal preparation for two months on seaming tracks in South Africa.

Without any consideration for the players in the Australian side this was agreed to, in a classic 'bugger you Jack, we're alright' manoeuvre. Why is it that officials and selectors are never accountable for their actions, but players are dropped for making mistakes?

The Board compounded matters by failing to insist on the very best accommodation whilst we were touring India. The players' anger then reached boiling point when we discovered the pittance for which our lives were insured on the tour. From memory, the amount was $400.

The final insult came on New Year's Eve, the last night in India before we flew from Bombay to South Africa.

For the Test match in Bombay we stayed in the primitive accommodation at the Brabourne stadium, where Doug Walters, in the interests of comfort, removed a couple of wooden slats from under the mattress. However, on climbing into bed he crashed straight through the flimsy construction and landed on the floor. This wasn't the ideal spot to get a comfortable night's rest before a Test, but it would have been acceptable if there hadn't been anything better available.

It came as an unpleasant surprise to the players when, on the final night of the tour, we were put up at the luxurious Taj Mahal hotel before flying out early the next morning.

The players' feelings of resentment towards the Board had

grown steadily on that tour. However, the ACB presented us with a golden opportunity to hit back, on the South African leg of the journey.

After a couple of victories in the Test series, the South African officials suddenly decided that an extra Test would be a good idea. Lucrative may be a better word, as they wanted to play a fifth Test in Johannesburg, the biggest centre.

The Australian team were approached with this proposal by Fred Bennett (the manager) and Bill Lawry (the captain). It was explained to us that the last two first-class games (against Western Province and Orange Free State) would be scrapped and replaced by a fifth Test. Then came the good news: the tour would be extended by a couple of days.

Why good news? It meant that our contracts had to be extended

As vice-captain, I told the players we had an opportunity to let the Board know that we were unhappy and sick of being pushed around. I suggested a figure of $500 would make them aware of our discontent, as in those days the fee for a Test match at home was $180. Graham McKenzie, Doug Walters and John Gleeson made it known they were firmly in my camp, and Brian Taber told me privately that he'd vote with us if it came to the crunch.

Following my comments, Bill Lawry made it clear it would be a case of either "all in or all out". The meeting broke up with nothing being resolved.

Then, during the third Test we were told that the Board members were prepared to pay $200 on top of our tour payments for the extra days involved in playing the fifth Test. Someone mentioned that the affluent Wanderers club in Johannesburg had made it known they were prepared to make up the difference between what we were asking and what the Board were offering, in order to ensure a fifth Test.

I became annoyed at this approach and said that the matter had nothing to do with the Wanderers Club and if we weren't prepared to 'stand up for our rights', then we deserved to be pushed around by the Board for the rest of our playing days.

One player in the 'yes' camp retaliated, saying he could use the money and that they should go ahead and play without the dissenters.

On hearing this I exploded. I pulled my cheque book from my back pocket and offered to reimburse him on the spot if he needed the money that badly.

Sensing that matters were getting a little out of hand, Bill Lawry stepped in and reiterated that it would be an "all in or all out" approach. With that McKenzie, Gleeson and myself confirmed that we were still of the same mind and the matter was dropped.

However, it wasn't forgotten. Back in Australia a few months later, Alan McGilvray told me a Board member had informed him that "Chappell will never captain Australia".

That member must have been out-voted, because in the space of six months I was appointed captain, following the sacking of Bill Lawry.

I then captained Australia until the tour of England in 1975 when I retired from the job. Twice in that period of four years I was invited to Board meetings to discuss any matters which the players wanted to put before the members.

In my first meeting I put the players' point of view verbally to the Board members. Following that meeting, Richie Benaud asked me how it went. I told him and he offered me some advice. "If you ever meet with them again, Ian, put your points on paper and give a copy to each Board member, plus the secretary."

I followed Richie's advice when I met with the Board again in Adelaide, before the third Test against New Zealand in early 1974. I made fifteen copies of my points and placed one in front of each member's seat, plus one for Alan Barnes, who was then secretary of the Board.

Ironically, twelve months later Alan was again in Adelaide, this time for the Test against England. He'd stated a few days earlier, in response to our agitating for more money, "There are five hundred thousand cricketers who would love to play for Australia for nothing."

Unfortunately for Alan, he was at the Wellington hotel for lunch on the day before the game in 1975, when a few of the players strolled in for a counter lunch after practice. A mate of mine, Gary 'Darky' Thompson, was with us, and when Rod Marsh introduced him to Alan, Darky couldn't help himself. He said, "Nice to meet you Alan. I'm one of the five hundred thousand, but I'm here to tell you I wouldn't be much bloody good." The irony of that meeting becomes clearer, when I explain what happened at the Board meeting in the same city some twelve months beforehand.

When it came my turn to speak on the points I had listed for each Board member, I couldn't help noticing Sir Donald Bradman's reaction.

He was sitting on my right a few seats away and for the first few points he sat back in his chair. When I came to the two matters on finance he sat forward, listening intently. After I finished each point he explained in his distinctive tone, and in no uncertain terms, that the Board couldn't entertain such ideas. After his little harangue (there were no more points on finance), he sat back in his chair and had nothing more to say.

Barnes, like many others on the Board, was a Bradman disciple and I'm sure The Don's attitude to players' pay was well supported. I think the policy of keeping match payments at a minimum contributed to the success World Series Cricket officials had when a couple of years later they approached Australian players with a contract.

That was the second time Bradman had made his attitude on rewarding players quite clear to me.

After my first season as captain of South Australia (1970-71) I went to Bradman's office just around the corner from the Adelaide Stock Exchange. I explained that I felt a couple of our senior players (Ken Cunningham and John Causby) were likely to retire because they couldn't afford to keep playing first-class cricket. I didn't feel SA was strong enough to lose players of such ability and experience, when they still had much to offer.

In preparation for this meeting I'd spoken to brother Greg's boss Colin Saltry, who worked for the AMP society. After I explained my idea of setting up a provident fund for the SA players, Colin told me it was possible, at minimal cost, to generate a reasonable payout from an insurance policy.

Armed with this information, I asked Bradman if he thought the SACA would be prepared to pay a small sum into an insurance policy, so the longer-serving players could be rewarded with a payout on retirement. I felt this would be an inducement to the better Shield players to play longer and would also bring SA into line with New South Wales and Victoria, which both had provident funds, although theirs only benefited players who reached Test level.

Bradman wouldn't hear of the idea. In fact, he wasn't even prepared to meet with Colin Saltry, and he gave me a lecture into the bargain. His approach would have been easier to understand if I'd asked Bradman to line my pockets with his own money, but I thought the request deserved some consideration, rather than the total wipe-off it received. A hell of a batsman he certainly was, but Bradman would have also made a great baseball pitcher. On matters of finance I'd struck out, two out of two.

However, Bradman and his followers on the ACB weren't the only cricket administrators who felt this way.

In 1972, Greg and I went to South Africa to play in the Datsun double-wicket competition at the Wanderers ground in Johannesburg. We'd already played in this event for two seasons and it had grown in popularity so much that they even had a team from Israel competing.

Robin Binckes was the liaison man between the sponsors and the players and when we arrived for the third year, he apologised for the payments remaining static. Robin said that Datsun were willing to increase the payments considerably, but when they approached the South African Board, they were told, "Don't pay them too much, because if you do, the other Boards are worried the players will demand better money for Test matches."

Stabbed in the back, eh?

After apologizing, Robin then told us that Datsun were happy for the players to charge everything to their hotel room and the company would pick up the tab. With that, we went downstairs to the bar, and Mike Procter walked up to the barman and said, "I'll have a gin thanks pal. A bottle of Gordons."

By expanding their horizons a little and liaising more with the players, cricket's administrators could have had the best of both worlds. The Boards could have kept their pay scale at a level they were comfortable with for Test matches, and then sanctioned other games organised by private promoters where the players were well rewarded.

That would have taken a lot of the pressure for higher payments off the administrators, while still allowing them to maintain control of the game. It may also have meant that WSC would have found it more difficult to sign players to contracts.

As it was, the players were fed up to the back teeth over pay and conditions—hence the willingness of Australian players to sign when a WSC contract was put under their nose.

But cricketers are only sometimes quick on the uptake.

At the commencement of WSC we set up a Players' Association, with the aim of having a strong body to ensure that players continued to be paid well as well as having an avenue to contribute to the improvement of the playing of the game. This, we felt, was going to be most important in the event of any compromise between WSC and the ACB.

We invited all players to join, including those involved in the Sheffield Shield competition. There was interest among the Board players and some joined, but, not surprisingly, most were worried about being seen to be part of a WSC-backed organisation.

However, with the compromise in place for 1979-80, we renewed our efforts to increase the membership to a hundred per cent of the first-class cricketers in Australia. There was still some reluctance on behalf of the 'Board' players, especially the two most important ones, Allan Border and Kim Hughes. As players with long term potential, we felt that gaining their signatures would encourage the other players to follow suit.

When approached, their attitude was, "We just want to play

our cricket, we don't want to get involved with any of the crap." I explained that as a member of the Players' Association, they would be free to play cricket and someone else would do the bargaining. When they were still unimpressed I mentioned that, unlike the players of the seventies who were only fighting on one front (against the Board), they would have two opponents. With PBL (Kerry Packer's marketing company) having a lucrative long-term contract with the Board, it was unreasonable to expect them to side with the players on matters of major importance.

I even put the proposition to Border and Hughes that they were less vulnerable as members of the association. The Board would never know how they were voting in that case, but in a show of hands by the players, the ACB would find out the result and it wouldn't take long to get rid of any troublemakers; they'd be dropped at the first sign of form loss.

Despite presenting what I thought were logical arguments, we got nowhere with Border and Hughes in particular and the Players' Association eventually dwindled.

However, it gave one last gasp. Before the tour of the Caribbean in 1983-84, the Australian players led by captain Kim Hughes were having a running battle with the ACB over contracts. After one particularly poor showing on the field (at the SCG), Hughes declared, "The fact of the contract issue not being resolved is not conducive to good cricket." Shortly afterwards, Kim suggested that they needed a Players' Association. I chuckled and thought to myself, "All you need to do is convince the young players of that, Kim."

Obviously that never happened. With Kerry Packer having been repaid the $10,000 he loaned us to help pay the costs of setting up, the treasurer Rick McCosker rang me about de-registering the Players' Association, which had been legally incorporated as a company back in 1979.

I told Rick I'd make a phone call before I gave him an answer. I rang Geoff Lawson, because I knew he was quite keen to get something going among the players. I told him the Association was incorporated and that he was welcome to it to save the setting up fees.

Geoff said he was interested and would get back to me. Apparently he didn't have any more success convincing some of the senior players than I'd had years before, and when I didn't hear from him, I rang McCosker and told him to wind up the association. That was done in 1988.

I guess the great baseballer Joe DiMaggio was right. Way back in 1940, after fighting a particularly torrid battle for a salary increase with the New York Yankees, Joltin' Joe was infuriated when the then Commissioner of Baseball, Judge Kenesaw Mountain Landis, entered the argument.

As Roger Kahn says in his book *Joe and Marilyn*, DiMaggio felt that the baseball powers were banding together to intimidate and humiliate a fellow who was just trying to make the best living he could playing ball. Joe told a reporter, "Landis is using me to get a message to all the ballplayers. Stay dumb."

The Judge would have been delighted with the opportunity to work with Australian cricketers.

The ACB used the Cricket subcommittee (which generally consists of the Australian captain and a number of senior players, plus a few Board officials) to fob off the Players' Association. Board members kept saying, "Why do you need an association when you've already got a say through the Cricket committee?"

I'll tell you why. Firstly, because any player who looks like becoming an 'agitator' at those meetings can be dealt with fairly simply at the selection table. And secondly, I believe the Board only make changes when *they* feel it's necessary, not because of the recommendations of the players at the Cricket committee. Otherwise, why is each no-ball in a Sheffield Shield match worth two runs?

Geoff Lawson assures me no player at the Cricket committee meeting was in favour of that experimental law, and yet the Board brought it in. I think it's a damned stupid idea, like most of the other changes we've had in the laws or playing conditions ever since I can remember.

When it comes to devising and writing the playing conditions and some of the laws of the game, commonsense and logic join Wilbur and Orville Wright and take flight.

While the best players are now reasonably well rewarded, there is not enough input on the running of the game in Australia from people with the knowledge gained from competing at the highest level. I can't believe there would have been as much trouble as there has been with our playing conditions in the last decade if the ACB had the benefit of advice from at least a couple of former International players.

In 1946, in his book *Cricket Crisis*, Jack Fingleton bemoaned the lack of former International players on the Board. Since the foundation of the Board in 1905, only eight former Australian players have gone on to serve on the Board. As you can see from the following table, five of those were born before the turn of the century and only one, Greg Chappell, was born after the second World War. Only four—Darling, Hill, Bradman and Chappell (all former Australian captains)—reached double figures in the number of Tests they played.

NAME	PLAY	TST	BORN		DIED	
Joe Darling	SA	34	Adl	21.11.1870	Hob	02.01.1946
Clem Hill	SA	49	Adl	18.03.1877	Mel	05.09.1945
Charles Eady	Tas	2	Hob	29.10.1870	Hob	20.12.1945
Claude Jennings	SA	6	Mel	5.06.1884	Adl	20.06.1950
Roger Hartigan	Qld	2	Syd	12.12.1879	Bri	7.06.1958
Sir Don Bradman	N/SA	52	Coo	27.08.1908		
Len Maddocks	Vic	7	Bec*	24.05.1926		
Greg Chappell	S/Qld	87	Adl	7.08.1948		

*Beaconsfield (Vic)

It is interesting to hear Greg talk about his period on the Board. He was not encouraged by some sections of the Queensland administration to become a member, and only decided to take the plunge when he was made aware that an Australian selector could join the Board if he won a nomination from his state association.

During his two-year period on the Board, Greg said, "I made

it clear that I was keen to offer my experience gained as a player and that I had no ambitions as far as administration positions were concerned." He continued, "Obviously some people didn't believe this for I had the distinct impression that they moved against my proposals on the ground that defeats I suffered would thwart any ambitions I had for senior posts."

However, he said, "Some Board members and Executive staff encouraged me to aim for positions such as Chairman of the Queensland Executive and Chairman of the Board, but that wasn't my goal, at least not in the short term."

In the end, Greg explains, "I woke up one Sunday morning in Devonport, on duty as a selector, and realised that my eldest son was thirteen, and in three or four years he was going to be finishing school and moving into the next phase of his life. I weighed up the choice between the aggravation I was experiencing as an administrator and the time away as a selector, or spending more time with my family. It wasn't a difficult decision."

Greg hints at the discouragement he confronted on the Board; that's nothing compared with what goes on if a former International wants to become a Board member through the 'normal' channels. After a long playing career he could easily spend another fifteen years, moving from the position of club delegate, to interstate delegate, to finally reaching the Board.

Surely a former player's knowledge and experience is most useful to the ACB in the years just after he retires as a player. Returning to Fingleton's thoughts in 1946, he says, "As a matter of urgency, the Board should set aside three additional seats to the thirteen (fourteen nowadays) now in being, to be filled by first-class cricketers on the votes of first-class cricketers, ex-internationals and internationals."

A laudable suggestion, but one that you can see hasn't been taken by the Board "as a matter of urgency". Sure, the ACB are guilty of negligence, but the players must also shoulder some of the blame, as they had their chance following WSC and could have achieved much more through a Players' Association. However, they've 'stayed dumb'.

THE WORLD CUP AND SOUTH AFRICA'S RETURN

"The Worst Organised of the Five So Far."

On the field I thought the 1992 World Cup hosted by Australia and New Zealand was a huge success. Off the field it came close to being a disaster on occasions and Imran Khan was justified in ranking it "the worst organised of the five so far".

Things got off to a bad start with the Official World Cup Launch Dinner at the Overseas Terminal in Sydney. The guests who paid $175 for the function received a marvellous view of Sydney Harbour over a pre-dinner drink, but in retrospect their money would have been better spent on a Harbour cruise.

Apart from the view, the long narrow room was a poor choice of venue for such a function. It lacked any feeling of a get together, rather like a rectangular dinner table compared with the round version. And the way the tables were set didn't leave an aisle suitable for a grand entrance by the players. To see the world's elite cricketers worming their way through the bunched tables like a Conga line wasn't a sight that had the guests on their feet applauding.

Then to deny the paid guests a word from the nine captains, especially with South Africa only just back into International cricket, was the height of rudeness. Instead, the crowd had to endure Ray Martin battling with a writer's jokes, when it would have made more sense to have him interview the captains.

But the worst was yet to come. The main speaker, former president of the MCC, Sir Denys Roberts KBC QC, totally misread his audience, if not his script. He 'died' early in his speech and would have been well advised to bail out quickly, but insisted on using all his prepared material whether it was appreciated or not. I could have understood it if Ian Botham and Graham Gooch had decided to walk out of this function, rather than the final dinner in Melbourne; the provocation was ample.

However, things picked up when the cricket started. I enjoyed the opportunity to watch a larger number of teams than in a normal season, and this also added to the variety of playing styles on view. The contrast between the cagey run-accumulating style of Javed Miandad and the uncomplicated, massive retaliation policy of young powerhouse Inzamam Ul Haq, was a joy to behold. The successful combination of these two extremely different players in the knockout stage of the competition was one reason why Pakistan became champions for the first time.

After a disastrous start to the tournament, Pakistan showed great nerve as well as skill in their comeback. They were worthy champions. Their victory over England in the final was a triumph for a skilled rabble over a well-disciplined unit. In a cricket world that is becoming more planned and less instinctive every day, Pakistan showed that it is possible for skill to win out over organisation, when one team has enough of the former and the other side has too much of the latter.

Pakistan's bizarre fielding would not have been tolerated in the England camp. For his part, Imran would hang his head in despair at times, but just when it appeared his team was coming apart at the seams, he'd throw the ball to Wasim Akram. In between the odd no-ball and the slightly more regular wides, Wasim would let loose a gem which was capable of terminating any batsman's stay at the crease.

Imran handled Wasim's bowling indiscretions with compassion and exhorted his champion bowler to ignore them in the quest for wickets. One can only wonder at how the regimented thinking of the England heirarchy would have coped with a similar player in their line-up, or if in fact they would have tolerated him at all.

The demise of the defending champions, Australia, was as completely unheralded as the resurgence of the struggling New Zealand side. The Australians flopped, while the Kiwis flourished.

The best clue to the topsy-turvy performance of the two teams lies in a quick look at the captains. Allan Border approached the tournament at his most pessimistic. He baulked at his team's deserved outright favouritism and warned of tough games against New Zealand and South Africa.

His worrying had an effect on the team. A jittery Australia, playing way below par and with a number of players horribly out of form, lost both those games. The side never recovered. And in what looked like a repetition of the mistakes made in the Caribbean in 1991, when the best balanced side was picked for the final Test after the series was decided, Australia finally got their batting order right for the last two games.

Martin Crowe, on the other hand, looked adversity right in the eye and defied it to hang around the New Zealand camp.

His opening century against fierce rivals Australia set the tone for one of the most amazing form turnarounds since jockeys discovered batteries. Having provided the inspiration, Crowe then grabbed the initiative in the field by opening with off-spinner Dipak Patel, in a daringly successful move.

New Zealand's upset victory over Australia gave Crowe confidence, and in a dramatic detour from normal policy the Kiwis adopted aggression as their mascot. This resulted in Mark Greatbatch launching a mortar attack on numerous opening bowlers in the tournament. While the Kiwi fans laughed, the Australian fans lamented, and if the Shaky Isles weren't quite living up to their name literally, certainly Eden Park was really rockin'. There's no doubting the return of South Africa to International cricket also helped make the 1992 World Cup a better spectacle. The addition of one more good side made the competition for semi-final berths more intense than in the previous four World Cups. In this regard, the change of format to a qualifying system in which each team played all others in the competition, as compared with the old two divisions of four, proved to be fortuitous when the opportunity came to allow South Africa to enter as the ninth team.

Even the harshest critics must have been satisfied that South African cricket had done its bit in a bid to break down apartheid. Despite all the hypocrisy which surrounded the sanctions, I don't think it can be disputed that the sporting boycotts had a positive effect in breaking down some of the barriers quicker than otherwise would have been the case. The time was right to stop beating South African cricket with a big stick and reward the efforts of those so energetically involved in the integration of the game in the Republic.

It is now to be hoped that, with the hand of friendship having been proffered by the cricket world, the South African politicians can be trusted to live up to their promises.

The appointment of former Australian representative Kepler Wessels as South Africa's captain, also added interest to the Cup. The Prince of Eastern Province has lost none of his determination and, in typical style, he led his team to victory in the opening game against Australia at the SCG.

The last time Kepler played first-class cricket in Australia it was in a Shield final at the SCG. After Queensland had managed to fail to win another Shield, Kepler took off his cricket boots and left them in the centre of the ground. When he was appointed captain of South Africa, I had the feeling Kepler wasn't just on a jaunt to collect his boots.

As it turned out Kepler damn near guided his team into the final. If it hadn't been for a set of playing conditions totally lacking in commonsense, South Africa could well have played Pakistan in the final. That would have been unjust, as England deserved to win the semi-final; they were only in trouble in that match because those same playing conditions didn't properly punish South Africa for failing to bowl their fifty overs.

And that brings us to the playing conditions for Limited-overs cricket in Australia. Since the game has become extremely popular in this country they've created more problems than they've solved.

The biggest scream over rules and regulations in the World

Test and One-Day cricket crowds at Brisbane's Gabba.
Test cricket urgently needs the attention of administrators.

England's John Snow was a great fast bowler who gave Australia a lot of trouble. However, he was on the receiving end at the SCG in 1970-71 after a bouncer struc the head of Australia's Terry Jenner.

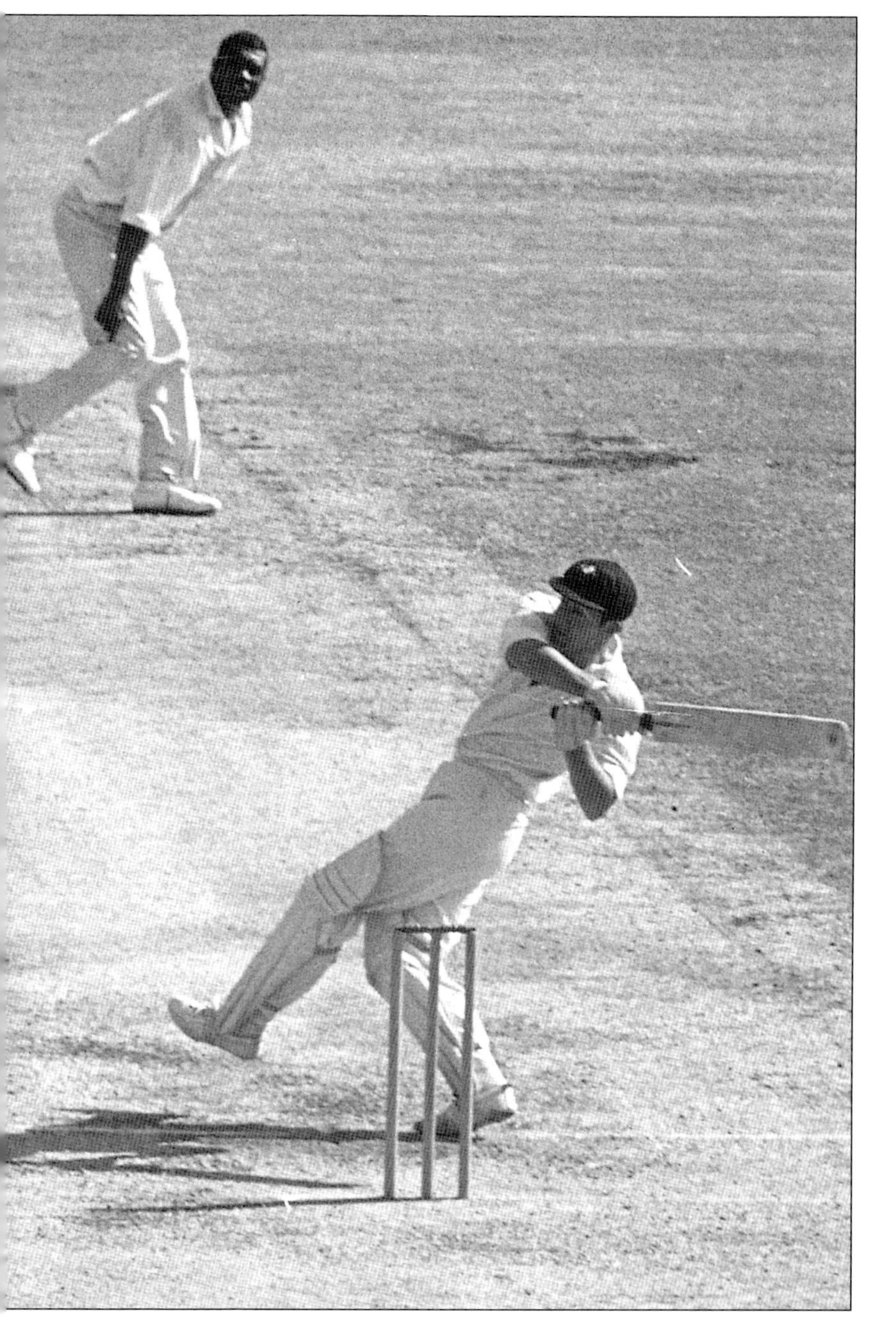

The West Indies have produced an extraordinary number of very good fast bowlers. Here Charlie Griffith tests my hook shot.

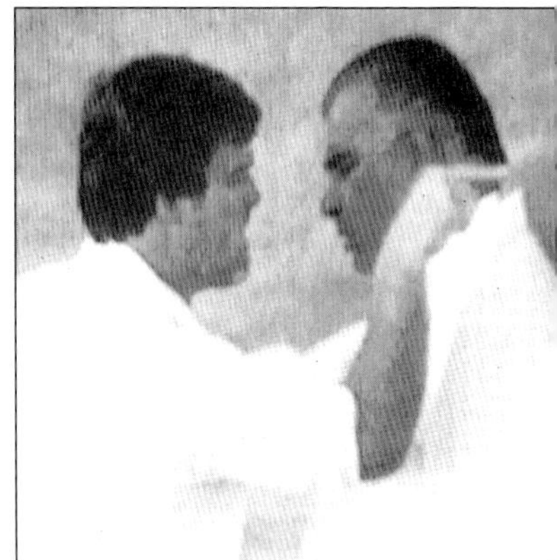

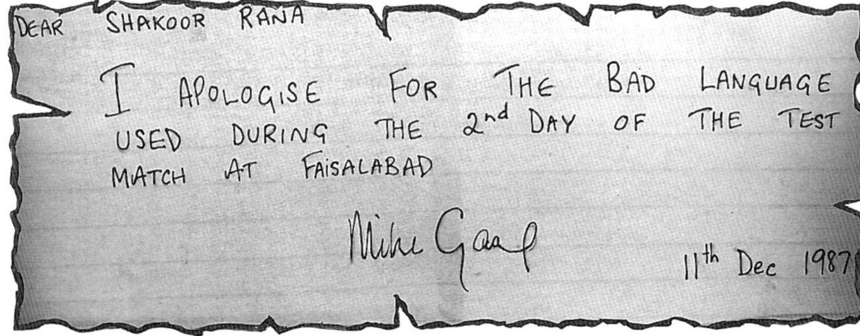

DEAR SHAKOOR RANA

I APOLOGISE FOR THE BAD LANGUAGE USED DURING THE 2nd DAY OF THE TEST MATCH AT FAISALABAD

Mike Gatting

11th Dec 1987

The beginning of the end for England captain Mike Gatting. His argument with Pakistan umpire Shakoor Rana was the underlying reason for his demise as skipper.

The Los Angeles race riots, 1992. America didn't heed the cries for help. The ICC has shown itself to be a poor listener, too.

The tour to South Africa, 1970, was a disaster for Bill Lawry's Australian team. Bill got the sack later, but the administrators who agreed to the calamitous itinerary survived.

On the two occasions I was invited to speak at Australian Cricket Board meetings Alan Barnes (right) was Secretary and Sir Donald Bradman a member.

During World Series Cricket days players and former Internationals made up a good proportion of the administration. Among them were Mike Denness, Tony Greig, Clive Lloyd, Garry Sobers, myself and John Gleeson.

Peace at last. Board members Ray Steele (left) and Bob Parish, two of WSC's most trenchant critics, with Kerry Packer after the compromise.

A good contest ruined by some inept administration.
The England-South Africa World Cup semi-final, 1992.

Despite claiming his first World Cup trophy, Imran Khan described it as the worst organised of the five held so far.

Cup came as a result of the formula for setting a target in a rain-affected match. In those cases, once it was determined how many overs could be bowled, the target score was the equivalent number of highest scoring overs of the side batting first, plus one run. In other words, if the second innings was reduced to thirty overs, the target score would be the thirty highest scoring overs from the first innings, plus one run.

This formula caused a great deal of consternation and caterwauling, because it was declared too difficult for the team batting second to win. The results in the 1992 World Cup don't support that theory.

In all, there were eight rain-affected qualifying matches. One was abandoned after only two balls, another because fifteen overs (which constitutes a match) weren't bowled to the side batting second, and in three games both innings were reduced because of rain. That leaves three matches in which the side batting first had a full fifty overs and the side batting second had to chase a target arrived at by using the above formula. Incidentally, one of the abandoned matches requires further discussion, but I'll deal with that later.

In the first of the matches under discussion, India, chasing a revised target, lost by one run off the last ball of the game. This game could have caused a heart attack in the commentary box, except that we were all laughing too much. In his commentary, Bill Lawry was exhorting Venkatapathy Raju to "run lad, run," but when he was finally out about a metre short of tying the game, Bill yelled, "Oh, he should've been running like a whippet."

In the back of the commentary box David Gower, with his slightly eccentric but quick wit, said, "What, on all fours, you mean Bill?" Apart from Bill and his co-commentator, everyone else in the box was falling about laughing.

In the second game, Pakistan, chasing South Africa's revised target, fell short by twenty runs after making a painfully slow start before rain hit the Gabba. The most difficult situation of all must be when rain interrupts an innings that has been commenced on the basis of facing fifty overs. The third of these games saw England defeat South Africa with a ball to spare, when they achieved a difficult target, with three wickets in hand. This was a brilliant exhibition of run chasing and another thrilling finish.

In the context of the overall tournament, there were thirty-nine matches, of which six were absolute thrillers. Two of those came as a result of the much maligned formula. Why then, was it portrayed as a formula for disaster?

To be fair there is the abandoned game between England and Pakistan to consider. On an Adelaide Oval wicket that was underprepared because of incessant rain, Pakistan were bowled out for their lowest ever One-day total of seventy four, off 40.2 overs. When rain again hit the Oval, England's target was reduced to sixty-four off sixteen overs.

There's no doubt England were penalised by the formula for bowling well. Of the twenty-four overs dropped to decide England's target, fourteen were maidens and only one run was scored off each of the other ten. Ironically, without the one point gained from this abandoned match, Pakistan could well have missed out on qualifying for the semi-finals.

Okay, that was one situation when the formula didn't work. But surely you shouldn't throw it out holus-bolus, just because of one frailty, when it has shown that it can produce good finishes in the most complex of situations, the rain-affected Limited-over match.

Apart from that aspect, the present formula does have another attribute. It is simple. This is important because the targets have to be easily and quickly worked out so that the players and patrons can always be abreast of the situation. It also helps to have a simple formula when rain causes a second or third interruption and everyone's patience is wearing a bit thin.

Another important consideration when striking a formula is to provide, as far as is possible, a fair contest and good entertainment. Therefore, you can't have a formula which reduces the number of wickets available to the side chasing the target. This could result in a second innings that only lasts a few overs, which is likely to cause a riot over entrance money and the loss of television rights revenue.

However, it is important to recognise that the side batting second has all ten wickets available in a chase which doesn't involve the full fifty overs. This can lead to the luxury of all-out aggression in a shortened run chase.

Recognising this and the hitch in the present system, why not incorporate these factors and improve the formula?

In the case of a second innings which is reduced to thirty overs, why not equally divide the overs into fifteen of the highest scoring and fifteen of the lowest scoring (with an uneven number the odd over counts as high). That rewards aggressive batting (especially not playing out any maiden overs), while also acknowledging accurate bowling. To recognise the importance of wickets, you then increase the number of high-scoring overs by the same number of wickets that the side batting first had intact at the end of their innings.

Using the 1992 World Cup final as an example, you would come up with the following figures.

Pakistan batting first make 6/249 off fifty overs. Let's say that rain then reduces England's innings to thirty overs. That means an even split of fifteen high and low, but Pakistan had four wickets in hand, so their reward is a split of nineteen high and eleven low.

Under that system, England would have been left with a target of 184 + 1 for victory = 185 off 30 overs. That compares with a target under the present system of 223 + 1 = 224 off 30 overs. That's exceedingly high when you consider in the early stages England bowled four maiden overs and seven where only one run was conceded.

Whatever formula is used, I'm convinced there'll be the odd imbalance. But the one that was in place for the World Cup in 1992 wasn't responsible for the botched up semi-final between England and South Africa at the SCG. That was a prize cock-up by the administrators.

Let me say first up that the result gained was the right one: an England win. It's just that it was gained at the expense of the game as a spectacle and put the umpires in a position of acute embarrassment. The officials who preside over such poorly conceived and poorly written legislation got off scot free, as usual, protected from accountability by their anonymity.

When rain hit the SCG, South Africa needed twenty-one runs off thirteen balls to gain a spot in the World Cup final. However, their chances of pulling off the biggest heist since the Great Train Robbery disappeared with the announcement that on resumption they required the same number of runs off only seven balls.

I was in the Member's stand at the time relaying the target to viewers on Channel Nine. When the public announcement was made there was much booing and shouting and a can of beer went sailing through the air, having been launched from the back of the Member's.

I knew it wasn't a good place to hang around. I was even more convinced a minute later when Alan Jordaan, the South African manager, told me there'd been a mistake and in fact they only had one ball from which to achieve the same target.

There had been a huge mistake all right. Not in the calculation or the formula, but by the officials. All that was needed was a simple message at the start of the playing condition saying that the umpires shall *do everything in their power to ensure the side batting second receives as many balls as the side batting first.*

With that as their main priority, I'm sure the remaining thirteen balls could have been bowled without violating any curfews that apply at the SCG. However, if South Africa had then won it would have been an injustice, as England would have been the victims of gross incompetence by the administrators.

South Africa only bowled forty-five overs at England (who scored a mammoth 252) and at no stage did Kepler Wessels appear in a hurry to bowl any more. How can it be fair for the side batting first if they receive only forty-five overs when they originally set out expecting to receive fifty? If the officials can't see the advantage gained by the side batting second in that case, then they shouldn't be involved with the game of cricket.

Surely a stiff penalty is in order. All they need do is multiply the uncompleted number of overs by the run rate for the innings and add those runs to the score, to ascertain the offending side's target. Then, to ensure the message sinks in, only allow the side batting second to face the same number of overs as they had completed when the allotted time was up.

In the case of the semi-final at the SCG, England made 252 off forty-five overs, which means an adjustment of (5 overs x 5.6 run rate) twenty-eight, taking South Africa's target to 281 for victory off only forty-five overs. This playing condition applies in Australian domestic Limited-over cricket and applied Internationally it would soon put a stop to any captain who harbours thoughts of malpractice.

Mind you, it does require forthright umpiring so that the batting side doesn't unduly waste time. Also, the same penalties must apply when the team bowling second is tardy.

However, if you think the semi-final at the SCG was a monumental balls-up, it could have got worse. The reserve day clauses for the semis and final were a formula for absolute disaster.

Let's not mess around with semi-finals. Let's go straight to the final. This is what could have happened.

England and Pakistan qualified for the final with wins in the semi-finals. Because England finished two points ahead of Pakistan at the completion of the qualifying rounds, in the event of a no result England would win the World Cup. But not to worry, the officials have wisely made provisions with two reserve dates (both day/night fixtures) immediately following the final on Wednesday, 25 March.

Let's say that Pakistan win the toss and bat and make 6/249 off fifty overs (as they did). Pakistan then have England struggling at 5/43 after twenty-two overs, when a huge storm hits the MCG. No further play is possible, and because the side batting second didn't receive twenty-five overs, the match is incomplete. Okay, you say, come back tomorrow and the game resumes. Sure, but at what score?

"It's bloody obvious," I hear you say, "resume at the close of play score."

Uh, uh. Under the rules for the World Cup 1992, you start again. Yes, that's right, Pakistan 0/0 v. England 0/0.

You don't believe it? "What happened to Imran's fighting seventy-two and Javed's equally gritty fifty-eight?" I hear you ask. Yes indeed, what did the administrators propose doing with the scores from a game that was incomplete?

Try telling Javed, "Sorry mate, you didn't make fifty-eight in the World Cup final. The record will show you made nought, bowled Lewis, in the second game."

Alright, so they play a second game. Pakistan again bat well and make 236. Then a fired-up Wasim Akram comes out and unleashes a few thunderbolts and England slump to 4/37. But wait, this is Melbourne. It rains again. Once more they don't complete the specified twenty-five overs and even worse, it continues to rain and they can't re-start (yes at 0/0 again) a game on the third day or night.

Who wins in that situation? England of course, it's bloody obvious mate.

Surely, if you go to the trouble of having a reserve day, it should be to ensure that both teams face fifty overs. I'm sure if questioned, the administrators would say that re-starting the match from scratch is designed to make it a better spectacle for the fans and the television audience. They surely couldn't have been thinking of charging another entrance fee and boosting the coffers, could they?

But in actual fact a re-start would have the opposite effect, providing an anticlimax for most of the players and for all of the spectators.

When a player is mentally ready for a final, he can cope with a wash-out and with having to get ready again the next day. But I would defy any sportsman or woman to get ready for a final, have it almost in your grasp, and then have to start from scratch again the next day. A situation like that would provide the team that was almost dead and buried with a huge psychological advantage they hadn't earned with their play.

When a round of golf is called off because of inclement weather, the players mark their ball and come back the next day to start from exactly where they finished play the previous evening.

Imagine if they didn't have a rule like that in golf. How would defending British Open champion Tony Jacklin have felt at St. Andrews in the 1970 championship?

On the first day he made the turn in twenty-nine, seven under par, and then made a birdie and three pars on the way home. When the storm hit and play was suspended for the day, Jacklin was eight under par playing the fourteenth.

He came back next morning and made three bogeys to finish with a sixty-seven, but surely that was preferable to replaying the round. If you play well they shouldn't be able to cancel it.

Fortunately, the worst didn't happen in the World Cup final, but why do administrators continually leave themselves open to ridicule? They did just that with the appointment of the umpires for the final. I was delighted that the affable Steve Bucknor of Montego Bay, Jamaica, was appointed. He had a terrific series as an adjudicator. However, his partner Brian Aldridge of New Zealand was by no means the next best man available to umpire the final.

He gave a horror not out off the first ball bowled by a South African in World Cup cricket. If Geoff Marsh didn't get a thick edge to Allan Donald's delivery, then I'm a Dutchman and Van Der Merwe is Australian.

Aldridge didn't inspire the same confidence as, say, Zimbabwe's Ian Robinson, who remained calm and efficient throughout the tournament. The World Cup officials left themselves wide open to the cynical claim that the New Zealander's appointment had something to do with the fact that the Kiwis were co-hosts.

I guess Bill O'Reilly has the answer.

Some time ago I was talking to 'Tiger' and the subject of cricket administration came up. Bill said, "Ian, remember in the park, when two guys with more hide than skill appointed themselves captain and tossed for first choice?"

"Yes, Tiger," I replied.

"Well," he continued, "the guy who won the toss had a pick and then the other captain chose a player and so on, taking it in turns, until they each had ten teammates. At that stage there were usually about six guys left over," paused Tiger. "Those six were the coat minders. Well, the coat minders went on to become the ACB members," chortled Tiger.

That's when the problems start. When they stop minding the coats and start making the rules.

SPORT – THE BEST EDUCATION

"Just Like Your Bloody Grandfather."

I know two people who wouldn't have been surprised when I was appointed captain of Australia. My grandfather Victor York Richardson and my father Arthur Martin Chappell.

Vic captained Australia five times. I'm proud to be able to say that, apart from my mother, Vic and I have something else in common: neither of us ever lost a series as Australian captain.

In early 1969, when I was appointed vice-captain of Australia, Vic told me, "If you ever captain Australia, don't do it like a Victorian."

It was the third and last piece of advice Vic gave me on cricket. He died later that year while we were on tour in India, before I became captain of Australia.

Vic didn't mention any Victorians in particular, but I was in no doubt that he meant I shouldn't be defensive as a captain. I hope if I ever 'run into him' he isn't disappointed.

Dad was a good allround sportsman. He was an aggressive and highly competitive Club cricketer and baseballer. He was chosen in the SA Sheffield Shield practice squad for the 1945-46 season and headed the aggregates (with 501) for district cricket in 1950-51. He also played in the SA Claxton Shield baseball sides of 1946 and 1947.

Like many others of his era, he was probably left wondering what might have happened if he hadn't lost valuable years to the second World War. However, I don't think Martin wasted a lot of time wondering—he spent most of his time planning.

His aim was to have three sons playing cricket for Australia. I'm sure his grand plan was to have Trevor opening, me at three and Greg at four, and if he could have devised a way for the three of us to bat together in the middle, then so much the better. I know he planned for Trevor to pitch to me and Greg to play second on the baseball diamond, because he mentioned it to me a couple of times. He visualised the day when Trevor would throw a pitch which I caught and threw over to Greg, who tagged a runner trying to steal second. Pity help the umpire if a close call went in favour of the runner.

Come to think of it, Martin wouldn't have done anything at the time, because he wasn't a pushy sporting parent. But he would have had a chat to the umpire after the game. He was a fair man and he expected his sons to play hard, but fairly.

However, fairness didn't enter into it when it came to drinking the night before a game.

Martin liked a drink and even as kids we were offered a sip or two of beer if the adults were drinking. He said he preferred to teach us to drink properly rather than find us doing it behind his back.

If ever Martin and I went out on a Friday night before a game we'd always be the last to leave. When I suggested to Martin I had to play the next day he'd reply, "Okay, one for the road, then we're off."

However, if I went out on my own and was a little tardy returning home (which happened occasionally), he would be angry. I can recall a couple of occasions when he scolded me because I had to play the next day and added, "You're just like your bloody grandfather."

If Mum was within earshot I would be off the hook. "Don't you talk about my father like that," would come the angry retort, and while Dad had his hands full placating Jeanne, I'd dive into bed.

In recent years I have read a lot about Vic and discovered that we did have a lot in common. And the last time I went out with him, I realised how well known he was.

I'd won the Cricketer of the Year award in 1968-69, and the

sponsors had kindly invited Vic and Martin to join me in Sydney for the presentation. In all those functions, once the official part is over, a few gravitate to the bar for the unofficial (and usually most interesting) part of the night. This night was no exception. After we'd been chatting for about an hour, Alan McGilvray suggested we go visit Vic's old mate Alan Kippax.

Alan had worked with Vic for years, and he felt it might be the last chance the two would have to see each other. Vic thought it was a great idea, so we all piled into a cab, McGilvray giving the driver the street name in Bellevue Hill and assuring us, "I'll recognise the house when we get there."

McGilvray didn't recognise the house, so, armed with his hazy description, we spread out to search for Kippax's place. As you can imagine, there was a bit of noise as we shouted directions and instructions to one another.

Suddenly a window flew up in a house just near me. "Listen you noisy bastards," came an angry voice belonging to a gentleman clad in pyjamas. Suddenly there was a change in his tone. "Is that you Vic?" queried the voice.

After peering into the dark for a few seconds, Vic replied, "Is that you Robbo?"

"Gawd strike me lucky, Victor bloody Richardson," declared Robbo, who turned out to be an old mate of Vic's from the services. Before I knew it we were in the kitchen opening a bottle of beer, rather than being handcuffed and finger-printed at the local lock-up for creating a disturbance.

Over a drink Robbo gave us directions, and I was still shaking my head in amazement when Vic knocked on the door of Alan Kippax's house. You see, everywhere I went playing cricket, someone would come up to me and say, "Ah...so you're Vic's grandson. I met him..." and away the bloke would go. I used to think that most of them were making it up until that night we bumped into Robbo. That's when I discovered that nearly everyone *did* know Vic.

Vic Richardson was one reason why I had a chance of being captain of Australia—in a lot of ways I was "just like my grandfather". There was another factor, for which I have no explanation. When I was fifteen years of age I was selected in a training squad at the conclusion of the schoolboys competition in Adelaide. One day we had some coaching from former Australian and South Australian fast bowler, Geoff Noblett. During his session he took us into the Adelaide Oval dressingrooms, and as we walked down the stairs that lead to the players' gate and onto the ground, Geoff told us, "I want you to make a wish, then write it down and keep it where you'll look at it regularly."

That night I wrote down on a grubby piece of paper, "Captain Australia." I stuck it in my wallet where I noticed it occasionally; there were rarely any other notes there to distract me.

Twelve years later, when I received the call from Alan Shiell telling me I'd been appointed captain, I was in the Overway Hotel in Hindley Street having a counter lunch. When I paid for my two schooners of beer and schnitzel with macaroni (with a liberal sprinkling of Worcestershire sauce), I noticed that grubby piece of paper in my wallet. As I'd never had any conscious desire to captain Australia, I can't explain the coincidence.

I relate in the chapter on captaincy how I went about that task, but that's only part of the story. A hell of a lot more than that went into my formal sporting education.

Brother Greg and I had the best cricket education any kids could ever hope for. I don't include Trevor, because unfortunately for him our coach Lynn Fuller was past his active days by then, and when Trevor arrived at Prince Alfred College (PAC) they were playing against other schools, rather than in the second grade (B Grade) Adelaide District competition. I believe playing against grown men at a young age gave Greg and myself a huge advantage over Trevor.

So much of my attitude towards playing sport came from my father. I was luckier than the other two boys, because I was born in time to witness a fair bit of Martin's sporting career and I did so from close quarters. From the time I was about four, I was in the car with Martin every time he headed off to play cricket or baseball.

I was the bat boy (with my own uniform) for the Glenelg A

Grade baseball team, so I was on the bench with the players and right in the thick of things. In the cricket season I was either pestering Dad for his cricket gear so I could play on my own out behind the grandstand, or I was busy playing in an extremely competitive match with the other kids. At the end of the day's play I would be in the dressingroom sitting with Dad and the other players as they swapped yarns over a drink.

Martin always said the only thing that surprised him about my swearing was the fact that I didn't start until I was nine. Having heard most things that went on in the dressingroom or on the bench at baseball, he reckoned it was a miracle I didn't start earlier. "But," he would add, "you've been making up for it ever since."

At age five I recall Martin playing at Unley Oval, and that's where I met Lynn Fuller, the man who was to shape my batting technique over the next dozen years. We were sitting in the old wooden grandstand when Martin asked Lynn, "When should I bring Ian around for coaching?"

Lynn replied, "How old is he?"

"He's just turned five," said Martin.

"Now would be a good time to start," was Lynn's reply.

So from then on, every Sunday from October to March until I was seventeen years of age, I practised on Lynn's backyard pitch about a mile from our home.

I didn't ever think it was a chore, and I don't recall Martin ever having to prod me out of bed, or push me to the front door on a Sunday morning. I remember one stifling hot day when I'd been batting for half an hour (most sessions were about an hour) and I suddenly felt ill. It never entered my head to call a halt; I just held up my hand to stop the bowler, walked over to the edge of the pitch and threw up. A gargle of water and I was back batting again as hard as I could go.

This was not punishment; this was pleasure.

Apart from Dad seeking out Lynn Fuller, my other good break was in moving to a new housing area at about the same time. Not only did this take us close to Lynn's backyard pitch, but also, as there were very few other houses around, there was plenty of land for playing sport and not many other kids to distract me. I don't ever recall playing Cowboys and Indians, or Mums and Dads.

By the time I was going to secondary school, I had sussed out all the sports-mad kids in the area and we had our own playing field that comprised a cricket pitch, a football ground and a three hole golf course. Just across the Sturt creek we had a beautiful flat sandy area which was perfect as a baseball diamond, and we used to spend most of our school holidays from dawn until dusk participating in multi-sports days.

After a day at school I would pound out the hours on the back wall, playing cricket or baseball, or kicking a football around the backyard. Whenever I was alone playing my Test matches, Claxton Shield baseball games or League football matches, I would also call the game as though I was a commentator. Maybe I was preparing for life after sport or perhaps it was another example of being "just like my grandfather". Vic became a sportswriter and sports broadcaster on retiring from a very active sporting life.

By the time I was seven and in grade two, I was playing in the cricket team at the St. Leonards primary school. However, my first real lesson on sportsmanship came when I was eleven, and it occurred after a baseball match.

In my last year at St. Leonards we formed a baseball team, which was undefeated in the local District competition. This meant we qualified to play the winners from all the other districts.

Because we'd won the competition so comfortably we thought winning was just a matter of turning up. So you can imagine the shock I got when our first real opposition belted us all over the parklands. After losing the game I sat on the bench bawling my eyes out, and Dad (our coach) came up to me and said, "Right Ian. Take your team over to the opposition bench and shake their hands and say 'well played'."

I was having none of this, so Dad grabbed me by the shirt, hauled me to my feet and gave me a good solid shove in the direction of the opposition bench.

It's not a lot of fun trying to wipe the tears from your eyes and shake hands with your opponents. It was a lesson that has stuck with me, and ever since that time I've never had any problem shaking hands with opponents who have beaten me, or my team, and adding the words "Well played" or "Too good on the day".

I didn't say I enjoy it and I'm usually thinking, "but wait 'til next time," nevertheless, I think it is an important part of the process of learning from defeat. If defeat doesn't hurt, then I'm not sure why you're playing. But once the pain starts to ease and you admit to yourself that the defeat or dismissal was not the result of (a) "poor umpiring", (b) "gross good fortune favouring your opponent", or (c) "just plain bad luck", and come to the realisation that it was your own ineptitude, then you are well on the way to learning from the experience.

One mistake I never made on the cricket field was to handle the ball. That was the result of another lesson from Dad.

I used to play for the Under-13s in the morning and then score for Dad's team in the afternoon. By that stage of his career, Martin was captain of Glenelg C Grade and in charge of a bunch of young players.

The great rivals were West Torrens, and when one of their young players stopped a ball that was rolling onto his stumps with his hand, the lad was given out on appeal. Gordon Tuck was their captain, a bloke about Martin's age and he created a stink over the dismissal.

In the car on the way home, Martin asked me about the lad's demise and I simply replied, "It's in the laws. He shouldn't have touched the ball with his hand."

Dad replied, "That's correct, and I don't ever expect to see you out handling the ball." Consequently I have always believed there was one simple way to avoid that happening: never touch the ball while batting.

I was amazed when Dean Jones touched the ball with his hand in the third Test at the MCG against India in 1991. In my book (and without the aid of a television replay) it was an open and shut case. Jones was out handling the ball.

At the time, I wondered about the attitude of other batsmen to touching the ball. I didn't need to ask Bill Lawry, so I checked with Sunil Gavaskar.

I explained my theory to Sunny and asked him, "Did you ever touch the ball when you were batting?"

"Most of the time," said Sunny with a serious look on his face, "even when the ball was within a few centimetres of me I wouldn't touch it. But occasionally I would bend down and pick up..." he paused and a little grin came to the corner of his mouth, "...a piece of grass. Especially when we were playing against Pakistan. I knew there were one or two players ready to appeal."

We both burst out laughing. "Not Javed and Sarfraz?" I queried.

"They were the potential culprits," chuckled Sunny, "but after a few times Javed used to say *'Cello, cello gend uthao buddhe,'* which is Hindi for, 'Come on, come on, pick up the ball old man.'"

My next lesson from Martin came a few weeks later. I scored for his team, not because I liked it, nor for the 2/6d a Saturday that I was paid, but because having come from a school match I was in my whites and hoped I would get a game.

One day my dream came true. Someone failed to show up and I got to bat at number nine. I only made a single figure score, but was delighted with the fact that I withstood the pace of a fast bowler named Blue Ballantyne.

That night at the dinner table Martin informed me, "You won't be playing with the Cs again."

I was devastated and asked why. "Because you're scared. You backed away from one of Blue's deliveries."

Martin sure knew how to hurt. If he ever thought I was getting carried away with success, he'd punish me by not taking me to a sporting event, in the process telling me, "You're a big-head." But being told I was scared was the worst thing I ever heard from my father.

I once related this story over dinner to South African opener Eddie Barlow, who laughed and said, "Our fathers should have got together." Eddie had been playing Rugby one day and made what his Dad thought was a rather hurried pass as he was about to be tackled. Over dinner (a favourite time for fathers), he said, "Don't you like your name, Son?"

"Yes, Dad. I think Eddie's a fine name," said the eleven-year-old Barlow.

"Not that one," he snorted, "you can't call yourself a Barlow while you're frightened."

Years later, a lot of adjectives might have flashed into the minds of International fast bowlers when the bespectacled opener challenged them with his flashing cut shots and bludgeoning pulls, but I'll bet 'scared' was never one of them.

Not long afterwards I challenged Brian 'Bunger' Hurn, one of our school first eleven fast bowlers, who was hitting catches to the Under-13s at a pace Test players would have baulked at.

I told him he was a big-head and walked away from the fielding practice. Little did I know that just two terms later I would have to face 'Bunger' in a house match. Brian obviously remembered my taunt and gave me a fierce working over, which I managed to handle (with great difficulty) for over an hour. At the time Brian had just returned from playing in a State second eleven match, and as a thirteen-year-old it was by far the fastest bowling I'd faced. Chester Bennett, who became the first eleven coach the next season, saw my innings and in history class the following day told me he thought I'd done a good job standing up to the barrage. Maybe he told Martin as well, because Dad never accused me of being scared again.

Obviously this was all part of Martin's grand plan. From the time we were old enough to walk we played with a hard ball, never a soft ball. He said he didn't want us to be frightened of the ball. From the time I was about ten years of age Martin would throw short-pitched deliveries at me, using the rise where the grass met the turf halfway down the pitch, to make the ball climb steeply. I can recommend it as a method to teach the hook and pull shots.

I hope he afforded Greg the same opportunity, because some of our backyard battles used to turn into torrid affairs. If I thought Greg was out and he refused to go, he'd receive a few short-pitched deliveries which he had to fend off. As always, we used only a hard ball, and having a four year start on Greg, I would imagine I had a strength advantage when it came to bowling short and fast.

Still, Greg doesn't regret it. He told me later, "Anything I copped in Test cricket was a breeze after the initiation ceremony you gave me in the backyard."

I don't recall whether any 'words' were spoken between the two of us, apart from the arguments over dismissals and runs awarded, but my attitude towards gamesmanship was developed at a young age.

Actually being on the bench during an A Grade baseball match, I heard most of what was going on between the players. I guess that's one reason why it never bothered me when somebody had a go at me. It probably also explains why I preferred to have a go back, rather than turn the other cheek.

I remember one day when Martin was coaching third base. The guy playing third for Kensington was Les Favell, later to be my Shield cricket captain. As often happens in baseball, there was a bit of chiacking going on and Les, who played with his false teeth out, said something to Martin.

Quick as a flash Martin shot back, "We'd be able to understand you better, third, if you put your teeth in." Not surprisingly, Les was a little cool towards me when I first played cricket for SA.

I copped quite a bit of the backlash from Martin's career, especially in baseball. Being a catcher means you have to talk a fair bit and I recall Dave Roberts, a longtime State player who had battled against Martin on many occasions, telling me, "You're a cheeky little monkey Ian, just like your father."

As a sixteen-year-old playing his first season of A Grade baseball I took this as a compliment. I doubt whether it was part of Martin's grand plan, but having to fend for myself against men, some of whom had been stung by his biting comments, was a good part of the toughening-up process.

When I played cricket at Prince Alfred College in B Grade we didn't cop too much from the opposition, just the occasional, "you college poofter". However, in my last season I was captain and I recall Alan 'Alfred' Hitchcox, a fast bowler who only the season before was playing for South Australia, giving me a workout.

At the end of the over I was at the non-striker's end when Alfred, whom I knew from his days playing for West Torrens against Dad's team, put his arm around me and asked how Martin was and if my studies were going well. I told him Martin was fine, but my studies weren't. Duly satisfied, he wandered off to fine leg.

I thought that was the end of the matter, just a bit of a welcome from the fast bowler and that was it. Wrong. It went on for the whole time I was out there and as captain I decided it was my job to stand up and show we weren't about to be intimidated. This was a principle I adhered to when I became captain of SA and Australia.

The next time we faced each other, Alan was back in the A Grade side and we renewed our battle, both verbally and with bat and ball. On this occasion I made a century which I'm sure resulted in my selection in the State side for the first time. Playing against Alfred a couple of times had helped prepare me for first-class cricket, where there was plenty of short stuff and a bit of gamesmanship.

During that second meeting, Glenelg were fighting to avoid defeat when our wicket-keeper Des Selby came to the crease. Now Selb has never been short of a word in his life, still isn't, but on this occasion he wanted peace and quiet.

After watching and listening to the battle between Hitchcox and myself for a few balls from the non-striker's end, Selb came down the pitch and said, "Chappelli, it's all right for you. You can hook, I can't. Now shut up and stop annoying this mad quick will you."

Selb got his revenge a few weeks later. We were playing Port Adelaide at Alberton Oval and 'Harpo' Marx Kretschmer was the 'mad' opposition quick (they're compulsory). Harpo had commenced with the college poofter line and progressed to the,

"You're only here 'cos your grandfather played for Australia," stage. When I hit him through the covers for a couple of fours, Selb yelled out from the sidelines, "Don't hit him too hard, they'll take him off."

Thanks a lot Selb. The next two deliveries didn't bounce before they passed extremely close to my head. A couple of doodlebugs, as Wes Hall used to call them, "low flying, dangerous objects".

Having played so much of my cricket at Glenelg, with teammates like Des Selby and Brian Rundle, I was never going to be tight-lipped on the field. These guys encouraged young opponents to "Get on with it. It's not a five day Test", or asked "Is that a glass bat your using?" As a wicket-keeper Selb used to specialise in advice to young batsmen, "The best way to handle this Sincock is to get down the track and hit 'im on the full," being his favourite.

David Sincock was the biggest spinner of a cricket ball I've ever seen and had an excellent chinaman, which he wasn't averse to using. Not surprisingly, Selby holds the record for the number of stumpings in a season in Adelaide District cricket, despite David only playing a handful of games because he was away on State duty.

Saturday afternoon Club cricket could be a funny day. I have often said Selb was the best 'keeper in SA from one o'clock until ten past, when his concentration span ended. From there on the slip fielders were entertained with a steady stream of stories about what Selb had done during the week. Most revolved around his employment with Golden Circle, under the managerial expertise of Brian 'Tom' Rundle.

When Selby finally resigned from Golden Circle to take up a job in Brisbane, he made his farewell speech at the St. Leonards Hotel. During it, he asked Rundle, "Tom, how many blokes are you going to put on to replace me?"

Tom didn't hesitate one moment. "A fourteen-year-old paraplegic, Selb, part-time."

Playing for Glenelg was an important part of my cricket education. They were a competitive team, but playing with such characters taught me to appreciate the lighter moments during a day's play.

When you think about all the people, clubs and schools involved in providing me with the best cricket education one could hope for, it's an amazing combination of planning, good fortune and coincidence.

Firstly, there was the dedication and time willingly given by Jeanne and Martin, not to mention the advice passed on by Dad. Then having such a close-up view of sport in the early days, plus the opportunity to put into practice what I learnt, was very important.

The advice and guidance from Lynn Fuller was vital, and without the technique that he helped me build, Test cricket would have been only a dream. Then to go to Prince's, where the coach was a former Sheffield Shield captain who provided gentle encouragement and the Headmaster a former New Zealand Test captain who displayed an unbridled enthusiasm for the game, was a huge advantage for a cricket-keen kid.

Even when I was at primary school I got lucky. Jack Butler, the coach of the cricket team, must have recognised some talent at an early age, and when I failed for a while to turn that into runs, he didn't drop me. Instead he wrote to my father, "I'm sure the runs will come for Ian. It's a pleasure to see his straight bat, when so many kids look like they're chopping wood with an axe."

Added to that, the practice facilities and pitches at Prince Alfred College were excellent. The head groundsman was a Polish immigrant, Sylvester Fuchs, who was so keen to see everything was just right he even practised the local vernacular. "How are the bugger wickets Ian? Are they bugger good?" Sylv would ask as he sought perfection.

Then it was on to Glenelg Cricket Club where, apart from the characters (and good players) I mixed with, there was a curator named Pud Cusack who one year asked acting captain Des Selby what was needed to get the team into the semi-finals. The reply was, "Pud, you go berserk with the hose and I'll do the rest with the coin."

Pud was one of the long list of characters at Glenelg and the story of how he rolled an empty sherry flagon into the pitch is still folklore at the club. So also are the two pitches he prepared that Greg Chappell made hundreds on at the start of the 1966-67 season. As a consequence, Greg was selected in the State side and Pud proudly claimed, "I set Greg on the way."

There were a lot of people who set the three of us on the way to playing for Australia, and it's only when I sit down and write about them that I realise how wide Dame Fortune's smile really is.

It also helped that the standard had already been set by our grandfather Vic Richardson. After one of Vic's magnificent fielding displays in a Test match at the SCG, a *Sydney Morning Herald* headline proclaimed, 'Is Richardson Human?'

He certainly was and although he didn't get involved in our coaching, he gave good advice. I've already mentioned the bit about captaincy. His other two were, "If you can't be a good cricketer at least look like one," and "Don't believe anything in this game is new, it's all been tried before. It's like your old suit: if you keep it long enough it'll come back into fashion."

How true.

As I explained earlier, wherever I went during my cricket career you could bet I'd run into someone who'd met Vic. The most common occurrence obviously was in Adelaide and it usually involved details of 'The Pie Cart' incident.

Apparently, after a night in the studio broadcasting a Test match from England, Vic and some of his cronies decided they were hungry. They stopped off at one of Adelaide's pie carts for the infamous 'floater' (a pie immersed in a bowl of pea soup) and while the others were eating, Vic mounted the horse and took off for a ride around the streets of Adelaide. If everyone who has told me they were there was actually in attendance, then it must have resembled King William street during the Christmas pageant.

In early 1991 I was having a drink at the Hilton Hotel in Adelaide, after a day's play in the fourth Test between Australia and England.

I was approached by a strapping young bloke who introduced himself as Richard Correll, a cousin of mine whom I'd never met before. Dick is the son of Vic's step-daughter Judy. Trailing behind him was the smaller, but nonetheless adventurous, Billy Wallace, a son of Vic's other step-daughter Maxine.

Over a beer, we discussed Vic and I mentioned the pie cart story. They'd never heard about it, so that gave me an idea. "Why don't we have a re-enactment?" I suggested.

They both thought it was a wonderful idea. So, accompanied by a mate of mine, Gary Thompson, we headed for the pie cart near the GPO. The owner of the cart happily agreed to our request when we told him the story and that's how we rode the streets of Adelaide in a Cowley's pie cart.

If Martin had been alive, I can just imagine his response on hearing of my exploits. "You're just like your bloody grandfather."

THE ART OF CAPTAINCY

"A Well-Trained Collie Dog Could do the Job..."

On the 1968 tour of England, a few of us were chatting in a bar in Kent when out of the blue the Australian team manager Bob Parish said, "Ian, if you don't curb your swearing, you'll never captain Australia."

I was amazed. Firstly, because Bob didn't normally spend much time in the bar and secondly, because I'd never considered myself a candidate to captain Australia.

I was so shocked I blurted out, "Well Bob, I've been swearing since I was nine and I don't see any point in stopping now, because I don't expect to captain Australia."

Even though I established myself as a Test player on that tour and by the 1968-69 season had been appointed vice-captain of the Australian team, it was still a hell of a shock to me in 1970-71 when I was appointed captain, following the sacking of Bill Lawry. Because of a number of occurrences, most of which are related in this book, I didn't think I was a unanimous choice as captain of Australia, either among Board members, or selectors.

However, I never knew for sure who was behind my appointment to the captaincy. I had the opportunity to find out not long after I retired from cricket in 1980.

I had played a game of golf at Pennant Hills with former teammates Brian Taber and Graeme Watson. Neil Harvey, one of Australia's best batsmen who was also a selector during my captaincy reign, was the fourth player in our group.

After golf, I chose an appropriate time (it must have been late because Taber and Watson had left), to ask Neil who was responsible for my selection for the captaincy.

"Me. Bloody me, that's who," came Harvey's typically forthright reply.

It gave me the opportunity to thank a man who many people believe would have been a great captain of Australia, but who, sadly, only once did the job, which resulted in a victory at Lord's in 1961.

Having finally discovered who got me the job, let me explain my approach to the task as I saw it in 1970-71.

The first thing I did was to list all the things I liked about the work of the three captains I had played under, Les Favell (SA), Bob Simpson and Bill Lawry (Australia). I endeavoured to incorporate those things in my captaincy.

Then I listed all the things I didn't like about their captaincy and made a mental note to avoid those traps. Then I decided it was important to stamp my own personality on the job. I figured if I was going to get the kick in the backside if it went wrong, then I might as well be totally responsible for the decisions that were made. Captaincy by committee does not work in my book.

Next, I looked at the team's performance. As the Australian team had just gone nine Tests without winning under Bill Lawry, I reasoned that if we continued to play poorly I wouldn't cop excessive flak. I thought the general reaction would be, "Lawry couldn't win with this mob, so how can we expect Chappell to change things."

Nevertheless, I felt an Australian victory under my captaincy would change things dramatically. I reckoned that would have the public thinking I was a genius (I wasn't expecting to fool Neil Harvey so easily). To me, a win was going to buy me some time in the job and give me a chance to prove myself as a captain.

My conclusion: I was in a position where I couldn't lose, so the trick was to win a Test quickly.

We promptly lost my first two Tests as captain. Fortunately we won at the third attempt and that amazing victory at Lord's, which will forever be known as 'Massie's Match', was the turning point in my captaincy career.

That was the game that gave me some breathing space. Incidentally, it must have also convinced someone I *was* a genius because the team was contracted to cut a record.

How anyone could believe I could turn that motley crew into a bunch of crooners, especially at three o'clock in the morning after a celebratory dinner, was beyond me. Just to prove that P.T. Barnum was right, the record 'Here Come the Aussies' and 'Bowl a Ball Swing a Bat', reached number one in some states of Australia. Yes P.T., there is one born every minute.

However, this musical success didn't derail our train of thought and we went on to win the last Test of the '72 series at The Oval. It was this victory which gave me the chance to qualify for an Australian captain's pension.

After completing the Test at The Oval three years later, I retired from the Australian captaincy. In that period I learned a lot about being in charge of a cricket team.

Like everything else in life, the most important quality to bring to the task is commonsense.

Whilst I don't agree with my old mate Bill 'Tiger' O'Reilly that "a well-trained collie dog could do the job", I equally don't agree with those who suggest that only a budding brain surgeon has the capacity to lead his country at cricket successfully.

Apart from possessing commonsense, a captain must win the respect of his team. This has to be achieved in three categories: as a player, as a captain and as a human being.

Under the Australian system in which the captain is selected from the eleven, he should have achieved the first aim, by being a longtime and effective member of the team before he's appointed.

To achieve the second aim requires a good knowledge of the game and of human nature. You must also be prepared to devote a lot of time to the job.

The third is a matter of being honest with the team and remaining basically the same person you were as a player. In his period as captain Kim Hughes often said, "You can't be one of the boys and be a good captain." That's rubbish.

Richie Benaud always adds that you need a bit of luck to succeed as a captain. I agree, but I also concur with South African golfer Gary Player, who said, "It's amazing. The harder I work, the luckier I get."

I split captaincy into two categories. Firstly, there's the on-field activities, which include changing the bowlers, moving the field and pinning the batting order on the door. At any one time there should be at least half a dozen members of the Australian team who can do this job without a hitch, along with a few clever collies. Then there's leadership. That's where the captain attends to his off-field duties, and I'm not referring to making speeches and meeting people at cocktail parties. I'm talking about time spent with the players.

This can involve the captain in anything from a chin wag in the dressingroom or at the bar, to a quiet dinner with a player to try and solve a cricket, or personal, problem. That's where the captain gets to know his players better and conversely the players get to know their leader.

I recall my grandfather being critical of Ian Craig's selection for England in 1953 at the age of seventeen. He thought it was making life difficult for the captain Lindsay Hassett. "What's Lindsay going to do," queried Vic, "if the young man has a problem. Buy him an ice-cream and sit down and have a chat in a milk bar?"

The amount of time a captain invests in off-field leadership is repaid in the form of lucrative on-field dividends.

Communicating with your players is vital and I believe they should always know what's expected of them. One of the joys of leadership is assessing the character of each of your players and then going about the task of getting the best out of them. That's where a captain needs to be an amateur psychologist.

When I took over the Australian captaincy, one of my first tasks was to tell Doug Walters to play his natural game, no matter what the situation. I didn't want Doug to ever be in two minds when he was batting. An aggressive player like Doug needs to be free of any thoughts like, "Will the captain kick me up the bum if I get out playing shots?"

Doug knew he could play freely without experiencing any recourse from me. His ability to counter-attack when the team was in trouble played a large part in at least two Australian Test victories I can recall.

In Doug's case it was simply a matter of him being told what was expected of him. Other cases were a little more complicated. Like Lennie Pascoe's.

In 1979 the WSC Australians toured the Caribbean. We had Dennis Lillee and Jeff Thomson to spearhead the attack, but I wasn't sure who was going to come through as the third paceman on what can often be heartbreaking tracks.

Our first practice was held at an army barracks, called Up Camp just down the road from Sabina Park in Kingston, Jamaica. It was a typically stinking hot day and the quickies were all working hard, with one exception.

Every time I looked around Lennie was standing in the shade of the palm trees talking to the locals. Each time I'd call Len up to have a bowl, he'd deliver a few quickish ones and then disappear back to the shade of the trees.

I didn't believe in haranguing players in front of their teammates. So that night at a cocktail party, I waited until Lennie and I were alone and said, "Who booked your tour, Len? Jet Set?"

"What do you mean?" growled Len.

"We're not here for a holiday Lennie," I replied.

"I don't like little psychological games," he protested. "You just tell me what you want and I'll do it."

"Okay Len, that's fine by me. You work hard and bowl fast and there's a spot in this side for you. But," I continued, "you stand under palm trees at practice and I'll ring the travel agent and have you booked home immediately."

Len didn't look too amused as he nodded, "Okay. But," he added, "don't play any more little games with me." I decided it was time to lighten the conversation and tossed in, "Where's your sense of humour, Len?"

I might as well have unleashed a grenade, with the pin

pulled. "I haven't bloody got one," said Len as he grabbed me by the front of the shirt and lifted me off my feet.

With that, Bruce 'Stumpy' Laird, showing more courage than commonsense, tried to step in between us.

By this stage I was trying to stay as close to Lennie as I could. I figured if I was going to wear one, it was in my best interests that it didn't travel too far.

After about five seconds, but what seemed more like the Gene Tunney 'long count', Lennie suddenly let go and said, "Ah ha. I got you there, didn't I." Then a huge smile came across his face and he added, "See, I have got a sense of humour."

I managed a curt "I'm glad Len," before I headed for the bar in case it was only a passing phase. But, following that 'discussion' and a fiery net session in Barbados, Lennie became a hardworking and valuable member of the pace triumvirate.

You see, a captain's work is never done and it can be damned dangerous. It can also be exceedingly satisfying.

I was fortunate that I enjoyed a beer and didn't like to be rushed after a day's play. I put a lot into a day's cricket and it took me a while to wind down.

It was nothing for me to still be sitting in my cricket shirt with a towel wrapped around my waist two hours after play was finished. On the other hand, I've seen Bill Lawry not out at stumps, then shower, dress and head for the team hotel by ten past six. It was much more difficult for Bill to communicate with some teammates, because he didn't like to hang around in the dressingroom and he rarely visited a bar.

I learnt a lot about the mental side of batting in the dressingroom. As captain, I also discovered things about my own and the opposition's players in the same environment.

A leader's most important task is to get the best out of his team. I'm not going to tell you that a good captain can take a bad team and pull off a string of miracle victories. But he can improve the performance of an ordinary side.

I get really annoyed when I hear people say a captain can't do much with a struggling team.

I recall Bob Simpson commiserating with me in the South Australian dressingroom at the SCG near the end of the 1974-75 season. SA were last, as we had been the season before. Bob said, "I feel sorry for you Ian, it's hard to captain a poor side." He added, "That's why I retired as Australian captain."

I forgot to thank Bobby, as I was part of the Australian team when he retired as captain. But his statement became my incentive. Next season, I was only a player in the Australian team and was able to concentrate all my captaincy energy into improving South Australia's position on the table.

SA's win in the 1975-76 Sheffield Shield season was one of my most satisfying moments in cricket.

As a captain, I was never one for curfews. I believe it's best to treat the players as adults and individuals and give them credit for knowing what's expected of them the next day. If they don't know, then either the selectors haven't picked the right player, or the captain's lacking in communication skills. And anyway, there's always the ultimate curfew, the selectors' axe. If you don't perform, you're dropped.

I spent a fair amount of time with the team and I figured that when I said goodnight, it was probably a pretty good clue that it was about time the others called it a night.

The only bloke unlikely to take the hint was Doug Walters. However, I didn't mind Doug staying on, because he never let Australia down. He had his routine and he didn't change. I would've been worried if I discovered others who weren't used to it trying to keep up with Doug. As a sportsman, it's very important to know what works best for you.

I found over my career that I had a weight at which I was strongest and that's when I played my best. A couple of times I trained harder and became fitter, but in losing weight I also lost some strength. Feeling at my strongest was most important.

I also felt eight hours of sleep was vital. I would aim to get to bed at around 11:30 and I found I slept extremely well on a half a dozen beers. If you're in training, that amount of alcohol won't hurt; in fact it acted as a perfectly good sleeping pill.

One thing I dreaded was waking at four in the morning

before a game and tossing and turning while I thought about what might happen later that day.

On one of the few occasions it happened to me, we were playing the West Indies in a WSC Supertest at Football Park in Adelaide. For some reason I woke early and kept thinking about getting hit in the head by a cricket ball.

This wasn't the ideal preparation for facing Andy Roberts, Michael Holding and Joel Garner, but the thought kept recurring no matter how hard I tried to erase it from the memory bank. My troubled night must have helped me concentrate, because I made a century, but I didn't fancy that sort of preparation before each innings.

Two important considerations arise from that example. Negative thoughts and a batsman's concentration.

Negative thoughts seem to occur, no matter how positive your approach. In my earlier days I tried to fight them, but found it disturbed my concentration when I was batting. Thanks to a tip from Paul Sheahan, I discovered it was easier to follow the negative thoughts with something positive, rather than continually try to fight off the negative thoughts. This method allowed me to get on with my batting in a much more relaxed frame of mind.

I quite often found that on the days when it was hardest to concentrate, I made a decent score. Other days when concentration came easily and I was seeing the ball well, I would often be dismissed playing an over-confident shot. It's just as important to put a good shot out of your mind as soon as you've played it as it is to block out a poor one.

As captain, these are the things you need to be able to communicate to a young player. If he's in a slump you need to reassure him and help renew his confidence, then head for the nets to maintain that feeling with the bat or ball.

In that situation (with a batsman), I would relate what had worked for me and point out that most slumps were a result of unsound thinking, rather than poor technique. I would stress the importance of solving problems in the nets, so that when you were in a match, you were concentrating solely on watching the ball leave the bowler's hand.

How closely should you watch the ball? Garry Sobers, the great West Indian allrounder, told me he was able to pick the length of the delivery by the position of the bowler's hand as the ball was released. If the ball was released as, or before, the arm reached the perpendicular, it was going to be full in length. If it was released after passing the perpendicular it was going to be shorter in length. That's straightforward commonsense, *if* you have the concentration to watch the ball that closely.

Whilst a captain is busy helping other players in his team and ensuring he gets the best out of them, he must also retain his own form.

This is one of the things I admire about Allan Border's captaincy. When the team was going through a horror stretch, he never lost form as a batsman. If anything, he played even better when the team most needed it. That is the sign of a mentally tough person.

I tried not to change too much as a person when I was upgraded from player to captain. But there was one aspect of my mental approach I did change.

As a player, when you make a century you are excited. If you make a duck you get down in the dumps. That's a big swing in emotions and it can have an effect on your teammates, as they begin to wonder whether you're really interested in personal success or in the team doing well.

This is why I have the highest regard for what Richie Benaud did as a bowler/captain. As a bowler, it's hard not to get frustrated or excited, depending on how the luck is going. And concentrating on a bowling plan is normally a full-time task without having to also take into account the other bowlers and the team's interests. A batsman/captain is not subjected to those extraneous worries and emotions on the field.

Lyn Marks, a former NSW and SA player, told me that he reckoned one of the keys to Richie's success as captain was his ability to remain calm under fire. Lyn said, "It didn't matter if the score was none for plenty, Richie would just stand there in the gully with his arms folded looking relaxed. Then suddenly,"

Find Chappelli! A Test century is a moment to savour, but it can be a bit scary when you're engulfed by fans.

Martin and Jeanne sacrificed a lot to give Trevor, Greg and myself a chance as cricketers. They felt repaid when we all represented Australia, although never as a threesome.

Lynn Fuller spent hundreds of hours rolling his backyard pitch, then coaching and bowling to us. He rarely took a break.

The man who started the chain—Victor York Richardson.
Neither he nor I lost a series as Australia's Test captain.

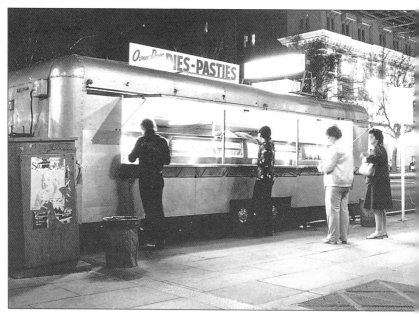

Vic did his bit to make Adelaide's 'pie cart' famous.
We had a family 're-enactment' in 1991.

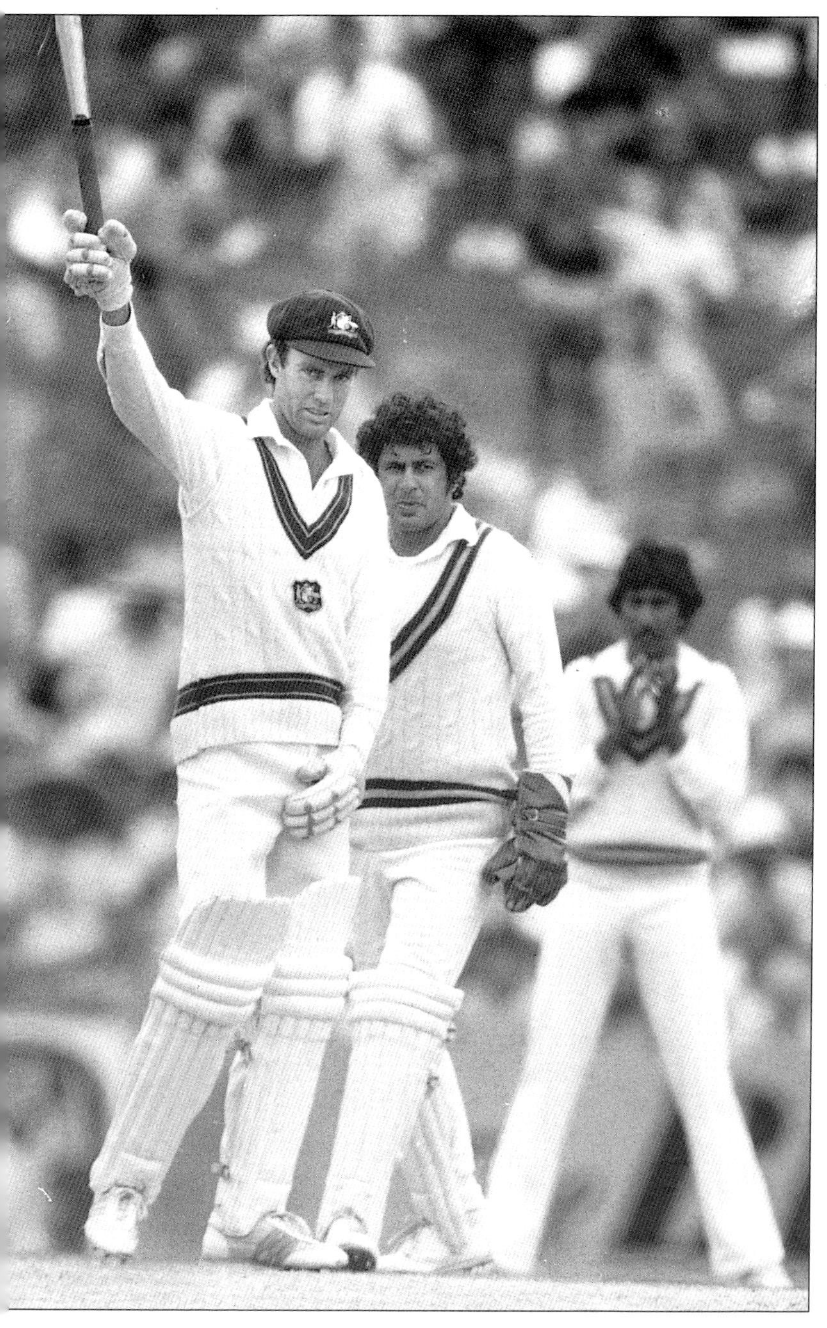

Greg ends his Test career as he started it—with a century.
Appropriate for a perfectionist.

The three captains I played under: Bill Lawry and Bob Simpson, opening for Australia, and Les Favell.

Bob Massie's match. His incredible 16-wicket debut at Lord's in 1972 set up Australia's first win under my leadership.

The two men who did a lot for batting and not much for bowlers' averages. Dr. W. G. Grace, Mr. Cricket in the 19th century, and D. G. Bradman, who carries the mantle in the 20th century.

smiled Lyn, "he'd make his move. A change of bowler, or he'd move a fielder into an attacking position and the whole team believed the game was about to change." It usually did, because the team believed in Richie as a captain.

I always tried to follow that policy when I was captain. Keep a clear mind and a calm exterior, no matter how much your guts are churning. It's amazing how fortunes can change if you can remember that.

You can also help yourself in this situation. Always, and I mean *always*, follow your instincts immediately. If you suddenly get the feeling that something is right for that moment, don't wait, do it immediately.

If it doesn't work out, then there's time to change tack a couple of overs later. However, if you don't do it, the timing will inevitably be wrong at a later stage.

Another adage that works in captaincy is 'Don't cry over spilt milk.' If a situation is deteriorating, make a move to try to change things. The longer you wait and worry about what's going wrong, the deeper in the mire you get. A good captain is at least a couple of overs ahead of the game, as a good snooker player is always a couple of reds ahead in a break.

This is why I think first slip is the ideal place from which to run a game. You can see how the bowler is going and it's also easy to check with the 'keeper on how hard a paceman is 'hitting the gloves'. First slip is the ideal spot when spinners are operating, as sometimes when they're not getting wickets, you can see they still have the batsman in trouble. Often you get the 'feel' that a wicket is just around the corner. If you're not at first slip then you have to rely heavily on information from a thinking wicket-keeper.

As part of my policy of always looking as though things were under control, I never asked my teammates if they had any suggestions. I figured this approach could trigger off the alarm bells and get them thinking, "If the captain doesn't know what to do we must be in trouble."

I preferred to create an atmosphere in which the players felt comfortable coming to me with suggestions. In his first Test Jeff

'Bomber' Hammond came to me at Sabina Park and said, "I'd like to try and bounce out Kalli (Alvin Kallicharran)."

My immediate reaction was, "Geez Bomber, he's a good hooker and this is a flat track." But Jeff was insistent, so I said, "Okay, I'll give you two bouncers and if that doesn't work, we'll go back to my way."

The first bouncer Kalli gloved to Rod Marsh and Jeff had his first Test wicket. As a captain, you never know where the next good idea is coming from; remember, eleven heads are better than one.

A captain must be like a computer on the field. He takes in all the information fed to him, but in the end he must spit out the answer. He must be firmly in control, although this should be done with a minimum of fuss and arm waving. If you're a good captain people will know who is in charge. If you're a bad captain, it's better the fans don't know who is messing it up.

However, there are times when a captain needs to put down an uprising. Graham Yallop had a problem with Rodney Hogg during the 1978-79 series against England. Hogg had taken a couple of early wickets, but after about four overs he decided his spell was over.

Yallop stood and argued with Hogg until the fast bowler eventually walked away, leaving the captain to scratch his head before calling up another bowler. This situation should never occur if a captain has earned the respect of his teammates. Nevertheless, Yallop handled it very badly.

If Hogg was refusing to bowl and the captain wanted another over out of him, all Yallop had to do was to put the ball down at the bowler's mark and jog off to his position without argument. If Hogg still refused to bowl, there was only one man going to be embarrassed and it wouldn't have been Yallop.

However, I always worried about Yallop as a captain, after he called on former football coach Ron Barassi to motivate the Australian team before a Test against England. As I read that, I nearly choked on my banana, mustard and cheese breakfast.

And when Kim Hughes was quoted in 1984-85 as expecting his team "to run through brick walls" to win the first Test against the West Indies, I was so stunned I thought I was the one who'd run into a wall. Never have I heard so much piffle in my life.

If you need to motivate an Australian team that is about to play in a Test match, then you're in charge of the wrong bunch. And when you're about to face the world's best fast bowlers you want your mind as clear and relaxed as it's ever been, not cluttered up with thoughts of using the hip and shoulder on the bowler whilst you're taking a single.

It was examples like those that led me to the conclusion that as captains, Yallop and Hughes had the same effect on the Australian team as the breathalyser has on office parties.

Although I spend a good deal of my life talking to earn a living, I wasn't a great one for speeches as a captain. A simple 'good luck' as a batsman left the dressingroom, or an equally succinct 'up an' at 'em' as we filed out onto the field, was about as near as I got to an oration. When a batsman is walking out the door, or the bowler's on the last of his stretching exercises, it's too late for a coaching lesson.

The only time a captain need issue instructions to a batsman is when there's a declaration looming. In this case he should give the players plenty of notice to avoid an out and out thrash and wherever possible, he should only be asking the players to do something he's prepared to do himself. Nothing undermines a team quicker than an average-conscious captain who expects the others to take the risks.

It is the captain's duty to ensure that his team is playing flat out to win from the very first ball. Only when the team is in trouble should he then resort to trying to save the match and, even in that situation, sometimes a well timed counter-attack can be of benefit.

Mike Gatting launched one such counter-attack at the SCG in 1986-87 when Australia seemed to be the only team that could win. With Gatting thrashing the ball all over the SCG, Allan Border backed off a little and it appeared England would at least save the game until Steve Waugh dismissed the England captain. It was a brilliant ploy by Gatting, whom I regarded as quite a good captain.

Any captain who plays to get into a position from which he can't lose before he starts pressing for victory, doesn't understand what an adverse effect it has on his team. The game must be enjoyable for the players and there's nothing like a string of draws to quickly dampen the enthusiasm of a team. The spectators might think they are the ones being punished by a boring draw, but it's also purgatory for the players.

Any player who fears losing is not a good candidate for the captaincy. That type of person usually finishes up with an ulcer and drives all the spectators away.

There's a big difference between someone who hates losing and one who fears it. A person who hates losing does almost everything to avoid it, but when it occurs, tries to learn from the experience. A captain who fears losing will do *everything* to avoid it, including not trying to win.

"Football is a game you play to win," said American professional team owner Al Davis, "otherwise, why do we keep score." Davis is right, playing to win is important. However, playing to win by fair means rather than foul is even more important, as an active conscience is a bothersome thing, both at the time and in later years.

If you look up the Wisden book of Test cricket records and its One-day International equivalent, you'll notice that all matches are won, either by a certain number of runs or wickets. That's why scoring runs and taking wickets are the most important aspects of the game.

If a match is in the balance and a captain is in doubt about what to do, he should recall that fact and take the more aggressive option. He'll be right more often than he's wrong. If a coach is in a quandary about whether the team should run around the oval or practise cricket skills, that slogan should come to the front of his brain in a blinding flash and there should no longer be any doubt.

Sure, cricketers need to be fit to play well, but being fit won't help if you're not proficient at batting, bowling or performing in the field. John Watkins, an Australian leg-spinner, was once arguing the case for running laps of the oval. He said, "I need to be fit to bowl overs twenty to thirty."

Fellow leggie Terry Jenner piped up, "Yes, but you also need to work hard in the nets to be good enough to bowl overs one to nineteen."

Captains should be regularly reminded that the best form of defence is attack. If you go on the defensive too early it's damned hard to regain the initiative. Apart from the fact that being an ultra-defensive captain short changes the team and the public, it also discloses far too much information to the opposition for my liking. It immediately tells them you're not really keen on getting involved in a contest.

By trying to win from the first ball bowled, you're giving the opposition a clear message that unless they want a real scrap they're in big trouble. That's why I like Tests that have a first innings score in the two-hundred to three-hundred range. It means the team bowling second have to be aggressive to get back into the match.

The 1972 series in England was such a rip-roaring success, because only once did the side batting first make over three hundred (Australia, 315) and incidentally, that was the only drawn game. With two victories to each side, it was the most exciting series I played in.

Only in exceptional circumstances (or if the team can score the runs in a day and a third) can I condone first innings scores of five hundred to six hundred. The idea of slowly piling up a big first innings score defies logic and is a good indicator that the captain isn't in search of a good scrap.

Unless Bradman suddenly strips for the opposition, the team batting first can't lose after piling up a big score in two and a bit days. This then forces the side batting second to play for a draw and, unless they bat very badly, that's exactly what the result will be; a drawn out boring draw.

I've played in some exciting draws when both sides have been attacking for victory one moment and then defending for grim death the next. These are the most exciting of all Test matches, except for the very rare case of the really close victory, or the even rarer case of a tie.

Garry Sobers was one of the most attacking captains of all time; a born gambler. However, one of Garry's gambles gone wrong resulted in some faint-hearted closures by Clive Lloyd and Viv Richards during the West Indies' reign of supremacy.

Garry, bored by three successive draws against an England team led by Colin Cowdrey in 1967-68, declared his second innings at 2/92 at Queen's Park Oval in Trinidad. This left England 215 runs to score in 165 minutes, which they promptly did with only three wickets down and three minutes to spare.

It is criminal that both Lloyd and Richards have hidden behind the shelter of the barrage of criticism that Garry Sobers received in the Caribbean for being, in their opinion, reckless. Allan Border is another who errs on the side of caution in his closures.

A declaration is when a captain dangles the carrot to give himself a chance for victory, but in doing so he automatically opens the game up for the opposition. A closure is exactly what it says—it closes one team out of the game.

These closures are nothing more than faint-hearted captaincy in my book, although the captains concerned have tried to dress them up by saying they use the extra runs to allow themselves the luxury of attacking constantly. If you strip away the bright outer clothing, you're left with soiled underwear.

When Graham Gooch and Mike Atherton were nearing a double-century opening partnership at the Adelaide Oval in 1990-91, I didn't see too many attacking Australian fielders, despite Border having set England 472 to get from approximately one hundred overs.

What makes these closures even harder to understand is that they come in an era when captains, through their experience in One-day cricket, are more adept at containing the opposition.

Despite the reluctance of most captains to 'buy' wickets by encouraging batsmen to play shots, they think nothing of giving a batsman gift runs so they can have a crack at his tailend partner.

I have even seen the ludicrous example of batsmen being allowed an easy passage through the nineties, while the fielding captain lazily pursues only the tailender's wicket. I'm proudly from the school of captains who believe you don't give an opponent even the most innocuous single, unless there's a well-baited trap involved. And you most certainly never, that is *never,* allow him an easy passage to a milestone, as that's just the time when a bit of extra pressure may cause him to err.

Also, never having played against Bradman, I performed my captaincy duties in the blissful ignorance of any batsman being 'undismissible'. However, had I played against Bradman and had the good fortune to be captain of a side with Bill O'Reilly in it, I believe I would have received the same answer from Tiger as I would have expected from Dennis Lillee had I requested he forget about trying to get Garry Sobers out and concentrate on the tailender.

I'm sure the answer in both cases wouldn't have been complimentary, but it would have been easy to understand. And I should add, well deserved. Let's hope we get an influx of bowlers with the spirit of O'Reilly and Lillee, who browbeat timid captains into believing that all batsmen are 'dismissible' and get rid of this largely futile and extremely boring facet of the game.

A continuation of the policy of combining timid captains with coaches who have a highly developed self-preservation instinct could lead to the day when a collie dog will be too well trained for the job of leading a cricket team.

COACHING – TO HAVE OR AVOID?

"An Australian Coach is Something the Team Tours England In."

Having benefited from excellent coaching as a youngster, I was appalled when I first read Bill 'Tiger' O'Reilly's opinion that all cricket coaches should be shot at birth.

I read that in the early 1980s. I've since seen it a few times, as 'Tiger' he is in name, but occasionally Bill becomes a terrier when he gets his teeth into a subject.

As often happens after reading an O'Reilly column, I started to think more about the subject. Whilst I would be totally unfaithful to the dedication and skill of Lynn Fuller (my coach) if I completely agreed with Tiger, I came to the conclusion that if you're going to have cricket coaching it should be very good, otherwise you're better off having none.

I think the second part of that statement is where the O'Reilly and Chappell graphs meet. The alternative to good coaching is to spend hours and hours playing and practising the game and watching good players perform, so you can *work it out for yourself.*

Having come from the bush, Bill O'Reilly is one of a number of great Australian players who learned the game that way. Other names that come readily to mind in this category provide an impressive testimonial to Tiger's assertion: Sir Donald Bradman, Stan McCabe, Doug Walters and Clarrie Grimmett, all came up this way and, when put together with the name O'Reilly, they would give even the most amateur of selectors a head start in picking a decent side.

Players who reach International level and succeed, do so because they have a certain amount of intelligence, as well as the skill and heart to perform in very competitive company. This allows them to work things out for themselves, seek information from players who have been successful and, most importantly, find out more about themselves.

That is one area that Tiger and I are totally agreed on: *The more you know about yourself, the better off you'll be in life.*

I was fortunate to have had a very good coach. I was doubly fortunate that he also had commonsense. And my luck was really in the day Lynn told me (when I was about seven years of age), "Ian, it doesn't matter how good I am as a coach, I can't help you out in the middle. So you'd better work this game out for yourself."

Consequently, I set about trying to fathom out things for myself and when I wasn't certain I either asked or watched. Adding to my good fortune, I had a father who regularly took me to first-class and Test cricket from a young age. My first memories of that experience are sitting next to Martin while he told me to "watch Miller. Watch what he does."

Australia's great allrounder Keith Miller was a great starting point and when he retired, I then followed the fortunes of Richie Benaud very closely. In later years, when I have wanted to find out something about cricket, business or life, most often I turn to Richie for advice. The best piece came when I was about twenty-one, when he told me, "Ian, this is a simple game. The simpler you keep it, the better off you'll be."

That wasn't the first time in my life I encountered commonsense, but it helped me realise what a necessary quality it is for survival. Apart from Richie, I have always enjoyed talking with past and present players and reading about the game. I have made some fascinating discoveries in this way, and I continually find out 'you never stop learning'.

The acquiring and passing on of knowledge is an underestimated value in a society where there's often an obscene rush to embrace new ideas. I'm not against new ideas, but I am also not in a great rush to push aside ones that have passed many stern tests.

The world does not need changes, what it is desperately looking for is improvements. In the case of the universal trend toward appointing coaches for International cricket teams, I don't believe this is an improvement. My idea of an Australian cricket coach is something the team rides around in on a tour of England.

The role of International cricket coach came into vogue in the 1980s. Rather than modernising cricket, I think it's put the cart before the horse. If Test players are so desperately in need of coaching, then surely young players aren't being properly prepared for the climb up the ladder.

I firmly believe that only the captain can run a cricket team. If he can't organise a Test side, or at most a touring party, then they've selected the wrong bloke.

I often hear that the need for a coach has arisen because an International captain has too much to do nowadays. Okay, I accept that there are more media commitments, and with a preponderance of Limited-over Internationals, there's much more cricket played, which means some delegation is necessary. But it doesn't mean you have to palm off the most important duties.

Only a captain can lead the way in building up team spirit and, with the help of a trusted few, plan the way the team will play. Only the captain can set the disciplinary standards required on the field and most important of all, organise the problem-solving off the field. Surely the added workload of an International captain means the more menial tasks, those that don't require someone with an active cricket brain, are the ones that should be farmed out.

In a reference to cricket coaches, noted feature writer Frank Devine even went as far as suggesting, after Australia's World Cup debacle, that "the future belongs to the hard-nosed manager who will develop strategies from the sideline and construct teams to fit the strategies uninhibited by ties of friendship and free of distraction from the need to repair his own footwork against fast bowling."

With due respect for Frank's writing ability I make these points. The most obvious strategies in cricket have always been planned before a game by the people who have to implement them—the captain and the players. When these strategies come unstuck, usually because someone in the opposition is on the rampage, there isn't time to wait for a guru from outside the fence to send out a new set of plans. The captain has to change things quickly (in fact, he should always be at least two overs ahead of what is happening) or the team is in trouble.

Anyone who can't 'read a game' shouldn't be captain of his national team. And herein lies the problem if coaches are going to be appointed all the way through the grades: How will we ever produce real captains if we don't force them to think for themselves from a young age? Captains do need some grooming.

Frank's point about the coach being "uninhibited by ties of friendship" should equally apply to his pet hates. If in fact Devine's scenario was the actual case, then how come Greg Matthews had such a tough time retaining a spot in the Australian Test side when he was quite obviously streets in front of Peter Taylor on ability? And why in recent times wasn't David Gower in the England Test side ahead of Allan Lamb, a man whom he's out-batted over a long period of years, and Graeme Hick, who is a long way short of even proving himself at that level?

Since the appointment of coaches there has been too much emphasis placed on conforming and not enough on performing.

And, if "the need (for the captain) to repair his own footwork against fast bowling" is such a distraction, how come Greg Chappell produced his best period of captaincy when he was going through a horror stretch with the bat? And why, when Border took over the Australian captaincy, was his batting unimpaired while he struggled to come to grips with the extra duties that had come his way?

And if you need any more proof: (a) How come Richie Benaud's record as a bowler was much better while he was captain? (b) How did Greg Chappell manage to improve on a fifty-plus batting average while he was captain? (c) How has Allan Border maintained an average in excess of fifty for well over a half a century of Tests as captain? And, (d) Why was my batting average as captain well above what it was as a player?

Cricket being run in the future by a coach from off the field like baseball is only a change, it's not an improvement. In an era when we are supposedly better educated and definitely better informed, suggesting a captain can't run a cricket team is tantamount to saying that the leaders of the past were smarter. The only way that can be true is if we deprive the present day captains of the opportunity to be their own bosses.

If you follow Frank Devine's theory through to its logical conclusion, it means we'll have coaches *running* teams all the way from District level through to the Test arena. Let me assure you Frank, there aren't that many good coaches around. Currently, we don't have enough to even cover the Australian team, plus the six first-class sides. Your proposal is another giant leap towards mediocrity at a time when we're already too far advanced on that downhill slide to contemplate increasing the speed.

The few good coaches that are around should be working with the most talented young cricketers, helping to properly prepare them for the top level. That's why the problem arose in the Australian team in the first place.

Early in Allan Border's term of leadership, there was a case for some assistance. The World Series Cricket years had taken a lot of experienced players out of first-class cricket and the District competitions around the country. Then, after the compromise (between WSC and the ACB), more International cricket was programmed, and so the young State and District players were still denied much opportunity to play with or against the best players in the country and also listen to them talk about the game. The WSC drain on experienced players probably had its greatest effect in the captaincy ranks at first-class and District level, which resulted in some inexperienced leadership in the 'traditional' game.

Consequently, when Border took over as Australian captain he was being handed players who needed help with some of the basics of the game, in addition to the normal requirements of a young player reaching International level. This was too much to ask of Allan Border, or for that matter, any other Australian cricketer, living or dead. To compound the problem, a number of experienced players were then lost to the unofficial South African tours.

In addition to trying to correct the problem with the players' basic knowledge, I think Bob Simpson's appointment was an ACB attempt to bolster Allan Border's captaincy. However, there was no sign of change in Border's Test leadership for three years, until that remarkable transformation in 1989. As well as a gradual change in personnel, I think Allan suddenly decided in England that he was the right man for the job and he actually began *running* the team. The fact that he still retains a coach is evidence that he's not comfortable with being totally accountable.

However, I believe those two problems could have been solved back in 1986, with about four weeks of travelling with Border and the Australian side. In fact, I told Fred Bennett that at the time the ACB were preparing to appoint an Australian coach. At this time of crisis, Bennett was the chairman of the ACB. I gathered the impression that Fred was desperate for another term at the helm and felt that if he engineered a change that resulted in victories for the Australian team, it would help his personal cause.

Fred did some canvassing amongst former players and on his rounds, he asked if I was available for the job. I replied that I wasn't, because of my contract with Channel Nine, and also because I'd had nearly twenty years of being on tour with cricket teams and didn't want to go back to that life full-time. I also added that I didn't believe a permanent coach of the Australian side was the correct solution to the problem.

After a bit more discussion on the subject, I walked away from our meeting convinced that all other candidates need not bother applying, because Bob Simpson was a lay-down-misere for the job. During the discussions, Bennett asked my opinion of Simpson's suitability for the job. I told him that if they must appoint someone to the position, he needed to be a person prepared to take a back seat and encourage the players to think for themselves, a person good at helping players prepare mentally, and wise in the ways of problem solving. I added that outside of helping players with their fielding and running between wickets, I thought Bob was pretty limited.

That opinion was formed mostly from playing under Simpson's captaincy and evaluating the advice he gave me and some of the other young players, but it was also updated by occasionally listening to his opinions and following his exploits.

When he was duly appointed to the Australian position in 1986, a couple of his early comments made interesting reading. Firstly, Simpson stated that he was hoping to quickly make the position redundant, by teaching the players to learn for themselves. In 1992, on the eve of Australia's disastrous attempt to retain the World Cup crown, he was re-appointed for a further two years.

Then he added that his appointment became necessary as the system had broken down "under previous leadership", because the senior players hadn't passed on knowledge in a way that was traditional in previous Australian sides.

I found this fascinating reading. On my first tour to South Africa (under the leadership of Simpson), I learned quite a bit. Most of it over a beer with Bob Cowper, or in discussions with Richie Benaud (a journalist on that tour).

In fact, one of the things that came quickly to my mind when I was appointed captain of Australia, was a comment made during a Richie Benaud coaching session on that tour. Richie had spent quite a few hours helping me try to improve my leg-spin bowling. However, on this occasion, he was working in the nets after practice had finished, helping Jim Hubble (a left-arm pace bowler) work on his in-swinger to the right-handers.

By this stage most of the team were long gone and there was only Jim, Brian Taber (who was helping me with my leggies),

Richie and myself left at the nets. During the conversation, someone mentioned that it was unusual that Richie, a former Australian captain who was keen on his golf, was spending his valuable time coaching, while the present captain was off enjoying himself on the golf course.

That comment was one of the reasons I always tried to make time for any player who had a query, or a problem to talk about, when I was captain.

I believe one of the disadvantages of having an Australian coach (especially one who is a selector), is that it tends to limit the source of knowledge that players can call upon. Why have one coach to advise all types of players on how to correct or improve their game?

There are a number of players, or former players, who are well qualified and willing to talk about their particular skill. A captain has a vested interest in obtaining the best advice for a team member—it might help keep him in a job. Therefore, if he can't assist a player, he'll quickly find someone who can.

On the other hand, a coach is well paid for his job and is less likely to call in an outsider to advise a young player, for fear of weakening his position. Who is he most likely to be loyal to, his livelihood or the captain?

In Simpson's case there are even greater problems, because he's also a selector. What player in his right mind is going to go to a coach and inform him he has a problem with his game, if he thinks this could cost him dearly at the selection table?

It seems fairly obvious that Steve Waugh and Geoff Marsh reckon it's too dangerous—their batting has deteriorated dramatically in the last few seasons because of obvious technique problems that haven't been eradicated.

One of the biggest drawbacks in having a coach of an International team is that the captain is deprived, to a degree, of placing his own stamp on the team. Even worse, in some cases the captain is also burdened with the coach's prejudices. Then, in the ultimate case of a bad appointment, a coach can cause animosity in opposing sides by either the things he does and says, or by things he did earlier in his career as a player.

While a coach is not restricted in his areas of criticism, the players are usually pretty circumspect when it comes to comments about opponents. This is dictated by the thought of constantly facing each other on the field of battle. Today's quotes may well be tomorrow's fish and chip wrapper, but they are also the following day's motivation for an opponent.

When it comes to a captain putting his own stamp on his tenure at the top, I believe that it is an important part of being a success. I got some good advice in that regard on my first tour as captain from our very efficient, but fun-loving manager, Ray Steele from Victoria.

Apart from not interfering on the playing side and contributing greatly to the harmony of the 1972 side in England, Ray also advised me in the first week of the tour, "Never forget that this side will always be remembered as Ian Chappell's 1972 Australian team."

Ray's words confirmed for me that I was on the right track in my desire to "do it my way". In other words I would accept the pat on the back, but equally, I would also cop the kick in the backside. As captain I was accountable.

While I reluctantly accept that a couple of extras are now needed on the payroll, one premise should never change. In an Australian cricket team the manager runs the off-field operations and the captain controls everything in regard to the playing of the game.

Fortunately, I only had one manager who wanted to trespass on my territory. He did so because he wanted to make sure "We beat the bastards". I told him, "We'll beat the bastards, if you leave the playing side to us and concentrate on making sure the cheques and the taxis are on time and keep us informed on the official functions."

I firmly believe that when it comes to coaching an International team, the best twelve cricketers in the country should be well qualified to do the occasional bit of fine tuning that's required. Apart from their qualifications, it's also good training in the art of thinking for yourself.

If a first-class cricketer is constantly noting the way his

teammates practise, it becomes second nature to look for weaknesses in the opposition when he's out in the middle. In addition, Australian players are continually playing against each other in Shield cricket, so they should notice any changes that occur in a teammate's game.

If, as captain of South Australia, I didn't notice any change in, say, Doug Walters' batting when he played for NSW, then I was an imposter. If I noticed a variation and then didn't check with Doug before we next played together, it would've made me a traitor as well. If the captain of Australia doesn't want the best ten players under him and all of them playing at the peak of their form, then the team is in big trouble.

Anyway, a lot of fuss is made of technique difficulties at that level, but I'm convinced that most slumps are the result of a mental problem, which then manifests itself as a loss of confidence. If that occurs, it's a job for the captain—it's all part of being a leader.

The best cricket coaches should be employed to spend time with the elite players from around age thirteen, fine tuning and forming attitudes that will allow them to survive and then flourish at first-class level. Those players should have had a good cricket education by the time they're seventeen, and whether they then succeed or fail will depend on what is in their head and their heart.

At the announcement of the opening of the Australian Cricket Academy, Ron Harvey, the head of the AIS (Australian Institute of Sport) said, "The job of the Institute is to take good athletes and turn them into world champions."

I thought to myself, Ron, you might have a famous sporting surname, but you don't know much about sportsmen and sportswomen. The important ingredient in a champion athlete comes from within, and without that, no coach or Sports Institute will make much difference.

BATSMEN V. BOWLERS

"Give the Bowlers Time to Take Twenty Wickets."

As I've already stated, if you look through the Wisden book of Test cricket, you will find that apart from numerous draws and two ties the other matches result in a win, either by so many wickets or a certain number of runs.

Apart from being a very important fact for all cricketers to remember, it also raises an interesting point for discussion. Who are the most important team members, batsmen or bowlers?

As captain of the Australian Test side I made it clear to the batsmen that "It is your job to score runs quickly enough to give the bowlers time to take twenty wickets." Spoken by a batsman, that could be taken as indicating the willow wielders are more important.

On the other hand, it has been a long held view that 'batsmen only save matches, it's the bowlers who win them'. That theory could well have originated the day Australian pace bowler Frederick 'The Demon' Spofforth destroyed England at The Oval in 1882, a performance that was largely responsible for the creation of The Ashes.

It would be interesting to put the question to a group of the great allrounders. In a roundabout way I broached the subject once, in the company of Keith Miller. Keith started out as a batsman, became a fast bowler by chance, and remained a potent force in both categories, taking ten wickets in a Test and batting at number five during his last tour of England.

On the day in question, Miller, Ray Lindwall, Neil Harvey, Rod Marsh and myself had retired to the ACB boardroom to have a drink after a function at the MCG. Miller, who was battling with a hip replacement, and Lindwall, who was recovering from having a toe amputated, both took a lift in a car for the three hundred metre journey. The rest of us walked.

After we were all comfortable with a glass of beer, I said to Keith, "Have a look at you two fast bowlers (he was a bowler for the purposes of my argument), you're both bloody hobbling cripples. Do you see anything wrong with any of the batsmen?"

Keith glared at me from over the top of his beer. "That's because batsmen never do anything," he replied, "I hate f...in' batsmen."

Keith's answer left me in little doubt about his priorities and also with the feeling that he wouldn't have been a pleasant proposition to face, especially when aroused.

However, I got a completely different reaction when I recounted the story to another fine Australian allrounder, Alan Davidson. "But he *was* a bloody batsman," exploded Davo, as he burst into laughter.

Batsmen or bowlers. Who does the most damage? The first thing you notice when glancing through the history of cricket, even before the 'Test match' became the measuring stick of a team or a player's worth, is that the law makers have done little to help the bowlers and a lot more to aid the batsmen. However, like one of those bottom weighted dolls, the bowlers keep on bouncing back up again, not exactly with a smile on their face, but certainly ready for another battle.

The first obstacles the bowlers had to overcome were laws to stop the graduation from the under-arm delivery to side-arm or, as it was often called at the time, 'high' bowling. As described in the enlightening publication, *Cricket in Conflict*, this must have been a gradual change, but never a peaceful one.

The bloke who deserves the thanks of all modern bowlers is a man of Kent, John Willes. John was by no means the first bowler to experiment with the side-arm style, but he was persistent. So determined was Willes to introduce the revolutionary style, that he threw the ball into the pitch and stormed off Lord's after he was stopped from bowling in 1822.

However, it was G.T. Knight, an All England player in 1827,

who made a telling observation. In a letter defending round-arm bowling, he wrote that "Batsmen have completely mastered the old under-arm bowlers and run-getting is steadily increasing." He went on to add, "The remedy in the past to the domination of the bat was to increase the size of the wicket, but there must be a limit to this adjustment."

Later that season when Knight, playing for Kent, and Jem Broadbridge and William Lillywhite representing Sussex, all bowled in the 'new style' some of the diehards proclaimed, "This noble triumvirate, like their revolutionary chums, have destroyed all hopes of ever seeing good taste adorn cricket society again."

As this has become a common catchcry in the game, only varied by the language of the day, one must assume that in the eyes of the 'It's not cricket old chap' brigade, a good game equates with the batsmen belting the hell out of a bunch of subservient bowlers.

Despite many law changes designed to stop the bowler's progress, over-arm bowling eventually became legal in 1864. By persistence and a refusal to be beaten down, the bowlers had taken the game to a new level. Obviously buoyed by these gains, some bowlers tried to take the advantage a step further, by chucking. This controversy raged until 1900 when "the problem of throwing was effectively ended for a period of nearly fifty years".

With the bowlers able to deliver the ball over-arm, it appears that the contest was held to be evenly balanced for some time. This is not surprising because there must have been some dodgy pitches around and they were also uncovered. Despite these advantages, the bowlers couldn't muzzle Dr. W.G. Grace, who was able to improve 'the technique of batsmen'.

The good Doctor was also a marvellous batsman, and he is credited with developing both front and back foot shots to deal with all eventualities. According to observers of the time, until W.G. achieved that level of excellence, batsmen had concentrated on playing off either the front or back foot.

Grace's skill was legendary. One of the finest bowlers of the time, Alfred Shaw, who developed an unhealthy liking for dismissing the Doctor and did it twenty-one times in all, described the Master's gift this way: "Well, young gentleman, it's like this," he's reported to have said. "I puts the ball where *I* pleases and Mr. Grace puts it where *he* pleases."

Apart from Grace, there were plenty of fine batsmen around, but the next one to take batting to another level was said to be Australia's Victor Trumper. Known as the Immortal or just plain Vic, he was proclaimed by most who saw him to be a batsman of great artistry, as well as undoubted skill.

In Jack Fingleton's excellent book on Trumper he tells the story of a meeting between Grace and the young Australian on his first tour of England. Appropriately it was at Lord's where the Doctor walked the length of the pavilion to seek out Trumper. On finding him in the Australian dressingroom, he said to Victor, "Bring me your bat." On receiving the bat, he then got Trumper to sign it.

Taking Trumper's bat, he handed him his own autographed bat and said, "From the reigning champion to the future champion."

The consensus of opinion seems to be that the difference between the two was that W.G. didn't have the beauty and style of Trumper. In turn, there are many who played with both Trumper and the man who took the baton from him, Don Bradman, who say that (as expressed in Ray Robinson's book, *From The Boundary*) "for all their admiration of the latter's skill, they decline to rank him as Trumper's equal for fascinating batsmanship, for imaginative approach, charm of stroke and all-weather attainment." The last part being a reference to Victor's widely acclaimed skill on dodgy pitches.

Trying to decide who is best out of those three, or any of the other great batsmen, is pointless. However, it is worth noting some interesting coincidences involving Grace, Trumper and Bradman.

W.G's last Test was Trumper's first and despite being born twenty-nine years after the Doctor, Trumper died the same year as Grace, 1915. Trumper made his first Test century in his second game, as did Bradman, and they were a similar age when they achieved this distinction. And in one for the numerologists, Victor Thomas Trumper has exactly the same number of letters in each three names as Donald George Bradman. While none of the individual names William Gilbert Grace has the same number of letters as Trumper or Bradman, in total all three add up to nineteen.

W.G. Grace's first-class career began at about the same time that bowling was evolving from a side-arm style to over-arm, with a bit of chucking thrown in for good measure. There's never a suggestion that W.G. was responsible for that change, but as his appetite for scoring runs grew, I'm sure the bowlers were glad that they didn't have to serve him up under-arm 'cannon fodder'.

Like Trumper and Bradman in the subsequent years, the Doctor didn't 'sit on the splice' when batting. All three liked to dominate the bowling, with Grace explaining, "I don't like defensive shots, you only get threes."

Despite his preference for domination, it appears that Trumper did have some sympathy for the bowlers and was often inclined to throw away his wicket after he'd feasted well at the run scoring table. In *From The Boundary*, Robinson describes an incident during the 1909 tour of England, when Trumper ran out Warren Bardsley for 219, made incidentally by four o'clock on the first day. Back in the pavilion, 'The Bards', as he was called by the team of the seventies, asked, "Did you think there was a run in it, Vic?"

Trumper replied, "No. How many do you want, Curly? Aren't you satisfied with two hundred? Others can do with match practice."

However, things changed in regard to run accumulating, even before Bradman commenced to consistently gorge himself at the crease, a habit which eventually led to the biggest revolt of all by the bowlers.

But before I move on to Bodyline and the part heavy scoring must have played in its appearance, it's important to note another facet of the game that was involved in the build-up.

In a book called *The Crisis in Cricket and the Leg Before Rule* (sic), first printed in 1928, the author, The Hon. Robert Lyttelton, makes a fascinating disclosure about Australian opening bowler Frederick Spofforth which helps to explain a change in approach to batting.

Lyttelton says that 'The Demon' Spofforth was in his prime when he toured England in 1882 and 1884 and took 404 wickets in those two seasons. Of those dismissals, incredibly only six were lbw. The lbw law at the time required the ball to pitch in line with and then be going on to hit the stumps in the umpire's opinion to gain a yes verdict.

That is a tough lbw law for bowlers, much harsher than the present one, but apparently it was not the reason for Spofforth's and other bowlers' failure to dismiss batsmen lbw. According to Lyttelton's book, it was considered unfair play in that era for a batsman to use his pads as well as the bat as a line of defence. So much so, that two players, Ring and Taylor, were accused of 'shabby' play when they used their pads to balls pitched outside the line of the stumps.

A table printed in Lyttelton's book shows that in county cricket in 1870 lbw decisions accounted for only one in every forty dismissals. By 1890 it had increased to one in seventeen, and by 1923 it was as high as one in eight. Lyttelton, with the backing of many cricket luminaries at the time, says that the increase in the number of lbw decisions coincided with a sharp rise in what was called 'leg play'.

Remembering that this book was written in 1928, Lyttelton goes on to say that, "The effect of leg play, and of course easy wickets, has been to drive bowlers to try monkey tricks, googlies and such like." Despite much agitation for change beginning from before the turn of the century, the lbw law wasn't altered until 1937, when a ball pitching outside off stump was added to the law.

Bemoaning the number of drawn matches of the time, Lyttelton goes on to add, "As long as conditions make batting so easy, the monkey trick bowlers will continue, because they get more wickets, but the scoring will be enormous."

You can almost hear the roar of Bodyline building up, as Lyttelton adds, "To show how completely the preponderance of the bat prevails, it is both interesting and sad to refer to Wisden's Almanack for 1928. Beginning on page 173 and going on to the middle of page 197, there is a wearisome list of batting records."

That was at the end of Charlie Macartney's career, a batsman who reportedly said, "Some cove's goin' to cop it," before he strode on to the Trent Bridge ground in 1921 and demolished the Nottinghamshire attack to the tune of 345 in only 230 minutes. It's still the most runs made in a day.

English opener Jack (later Sir Jack) Hobbs was nearing the end of an illustrious career that brought him one hundred and ninety-seven first-class hundreds, with his hundredth century not being posted until his forty-first year.

Wally Hammond of England was just commencing his period of plunder. Hammond made his first appearance in Australia in the same game as a young Don Bradman made his Test debut. In the second Test of that 1928-29 series, while Bradman looked on as twelfth man, Hammond accumulated 251. He followed that with another double century in the next Test match, a feat which must have made an indelible impression on a young Australian who already had shown a desire to punish bowlers to the utmost.

Bradman had been set a good example in the ways of mammoth scoring by Australian opener Bill Ponsford. He had a huge appetite for runs, and before Bradman had made his Test debut, 'Ponnie' had twice passed four hundred and once exceeded three hundred in innings for Victoria.

In fact, it's enlightening to glance through the list of the highest individual scores in first-class cricket and note how many of them were made in the period between 1920 and the Depression. The names Bradman and Ponsford feature regularly near the top of that list.

Following a double failure in his first Test and one game as twelfth man, Bradman really hit his run scoring stride. He made a hundred in his second Test against England and followed that with another in his fourth game. Then came the 1930 tour, when, less than a decade before the German invasion, Bradman blitzed England. It was a run scoring spree that must have seemed to the English bowlers like it was never ending and always ascending.

In his fifth Test against the old enemy he made a relatively sedate start with 131. Then followed a 254 at Lord's, an innings The Don has described as his most perfect, saying, "I only mistimed one shot." How many I ask, could he have mistimed in the next Test when he produced his amazing 309 in a day (105 before lunch, 115 between lunch and tea and a *mere* 89 in the final session) and went on to complete a then world record score of 334.

He must have taken a match to recharge his batteries and then compiled 232 in the final Test. Harold Larwood was an England bowler in all but two of that sequence of Test matches in Australia and then England. Is it any wonder he jumped at the opportunity to get some of his own back, when England captain Douglas Jardine introduced Bodyline in 1932-33?

If, as some who saw both men bat say, Bradman couldn't match Trumper for artistry, then he certainly took batsmanship to another plateau in regard to scoring heavily. When it came to run scoring Bradman climbed Mount Everest, and I don't expect any further expeditions to join him at the summit.

Not surprisingly after this battering, it was perceived that the bowlers needed help. In 1931 both the height and width of the stumps were increased by an inch to their present dimensions. This change, plus the addition in 1970 of the 'no genuine attempt to play the ball with his bat' clause to the lbw law, must surely be the only assistance given to the bowlers by the law-makers in more than sixty years. In that period, every other advantage they gained was achieved at the expense of a lot of sweat and blood.

Surprisingly, there was no immediate major change to the laws after the turbulent 1932-33 season, but there were plenty of heated discussions, which resulted in an uneasy truce over short-pitched bowling. Harold Larwood had struck a blow for the bowlers. However, in the backlash, he was the man who suffered most.

At the time, Bodyline created an enormous upheaval in the game and caused much acrimony, yet it also brought unprecedented publicity and record crowds. More than fifty years on, it can be looked upon by most, excepting those who participated, as part of the evolution of the game. Reading about the build-up to Bodyline, I must say I'm not surprised that it occurred.

Apart from everything I've already discussed, there are some other factors which must have had some influence on the bowling of Bodyline.

As in 1827, when G.T. Knight spoke out, it's not hard to imagine the bowlers becoming heartily sick of batsmen and teams churning out huge scores on good pitches. As a miner who had come out of the pits of Nottinghamshire to bowl for England, Harold Larwood would have been well aware of the miners' uprisings in that country in the early 1900s. In essence, his attack on the Australian batsmen could well have been a protest about the working conditions for bowlers. There's no doubt the message conveyed was along the lines of, "If you want to make a big score, you're going to have to be prepared to risk injury."

From the batsman's point of view it's interesting to note the reaction of the stylish Alan Kippax who played in the first Test of the Bodyline series. In a small 1933 publication titled *Anti Body-Line* (sic), he states, "And so long as that cordon of fieldsmen is placed along the leg-side neither Jardine nor his bowlers can deny the charge of bowling at the man. Let him (Jardine) place a reasonable field and Larwood and Voce can bowl where they like as fast as they like, and there will be no kick coming."

Whereas in 1931 the administrators came to the aid of the bowlers by increasing the dimensions of the wickets, on this occasion they acted in favour of the batsmen by removing the threat of Bodyline bowling.

Despite his highly dubious disappearance from the game,

Harold Larwood didn't go back to a life of mining. But short-pitched bowling was forced underground for a while, after Bodyline had one final fling. In the second Test at Old Trafford in 1933, the West Indies served it up to England, through the agency of Learie Constantine and Manny Martindale. They managed to unsettle most of the English batsmen and even cut the chin of Wally Hammond, but in typically determined fashion Douglas Jardine, the creator of Bodyline, made his only Test century in that match.

Incidentally, with all the furore over Bodyline, an important milestone in cricket history seems to have been partially overlooked. I have seen film of Don Bradman shaking hands with Len Hutton at The Oval in 1938 as the English opener's score passed 334. The reason being, according to the narrator, that Hutton had just surpassed Bradman's world record score made at Leeds in 1930. What about Wally Hammond's 336 not out in the second Test at Auckland in 1932-33?

With the exclusion of Larwood from Test cricket, it appears that an uneasy peace reigned in Test cricket when it came to the subject of short-pitched bowling. A good idea of the stand-off that existed can be gained from an excerpt in Ray Robinson's marvellous publication, *On Top Down Under*.

When Victoria's Laurie Nash bowled a few bouncers at the Englishmen before the final, deciding Test in 1936-37, England's captain Gubby Allen spoke to Bradman, who had taken over the captaincy for that series: "We don't want a bouncer war, but if this starts, we'll really turn it on."

"No, that won't happen," replied Bradman.

"Why not?" asked Allen.

"Because my bowlers are faster than yours and can bowl nastier bumpers. You know my attitude on this. I have never favoured it and never encouraged it," replied Bradman.

However, by 1948 Miller and Lindwall were a feared combination, and Australia had a decided advantage in the pace stakes (remember, when you've got 'em make the most of it, etc). Having suffered through Bodyline, it was not unexpected that Bradman would savour the thought of having the upperhand. As Ray Robinson describes, "He was no believer in other-cheekmanship."

But he goes on to add that Bradman's "wells of compassion had not entirely dried out". After an exchange of bouncers from Lindwall and Miller in 1948, Bill Edrich was rubbing an elbow when Bradman said, "I'm sorry about this Bill, but when the boys get a bit wild they are hard to control." Bradman then spoke to Miller.

This was in the same match in which English strokemaker Denis Compton (on four) mishooked a ball into his face and after treatment, returned to hammer his tormentors to the tune of 145 not out. Apart from being very skilful, Denis was always a batsman who looked for the aggressive solution to a problem, rather than passive resistance.

In a roundabout way, it could well have been the Australian combination of Lindwall and Miller who helped to shape the West Indies' attitude on fast bowling.

When I first toured the Caribbean in 1973, it was often mentioned to me by the locals that it was Miller and Lindwall who gave Denis Atkinson and Clairemont Depeiza a 'going over' at Kensington Oval, Barbados, in 1954-55. This was obviously something that had stayed in their minds, and as Barbados has been the head office in the West Indies' fast-bowling factory, it's perhaps not surprising that the next two models from there, Wes Hall and Charlie Griffith, gave the Australians a bit of their own medicine on the 1965 tour.

The next confrontation between Australia and England featured John Snow in 1970-71. He headed an English fast bowling squad that their captain Ray Illingworth had virtually handpicked. Like Douglas Jardine before him, Illingworth realised the worth of good fast bowling on Australian pitches, and his wisdom was rewarded with a two-nil Ashes victory.

In an attempt to combat Snow and Co., brother Greg and I spent three months of the following winter practising against the short-pitched ball. On a shiny cement pitch, using baseballs because they bounced more and throwing them at each other from about sixteen metres, we both sharpened our footwork and hook shots.

It paid off in England in 1972 and then in the following series of 1974-75, when we were better able to combat short-pitched bowling. However, the short stuff didn't last too long in that second series, because we had Dennis Lillee and Jeff Thomson on our side. There's nothing like extreme pace to convince the opposition fast bowlers that it's not wise to indulge in a bouncer war.

The irony of my captaining Australia against England when Dennis Lillee and Jeff Thomson were in full cry only struck me after I'd retired.

During the Bodyline series Vic Richardson was one of the Australian batsmen who tried to 'take on' Larwood and Voce by hooking. He also advocated a policy of retaliation when it came to the short-pitched stuff. He reasoned (and I think the quoted comments of the English batsmen bear him out) that a fiery response would soon end the exchange and there'd be a return to 'normal' cricket.

However, the skipper Bill Woodfull, a proud and principled man, refused to allow any retaliation; the Australians were forced to suffer, if not in silence, then at least in self-denial. I think Vic would feel that even if the ledger hadn't been squared in 1974-75, at least a few of the debits had been erased.

Following that series, the West Indies arrived in Australia with Andy Roberts and a young Michael Holding. The Windies were building up to more than a decade of domination with 'a fearsome foursome'.

By the late seventies the West Indies' fast-bowling factory was in full production and they weren't turning out standard models, they were mainly deluxe. This is about the time batsmen should have realised the wheel had turned the full circle since 1827 when Mr. Knight had said, "Batsmen have completely mastered the old under-arm bowlers..."

Clive Lloyd has often stated that the idea for the four-pronged pace attack came to him after he noted the success of Lillee and Thomson in 1975-76. Only once in that series did Australia employ four fast bowlers and that was in Perth, where we lost by a whopping innings and eighty-seven runs.

However, that didn't deter Lloydy, and his ploy was the basis for an unprecedented run of success for the West Indies.

Their success not only shattered a few batting reputations, but it also had a dulling effect on the collective cricketing brains of the world. Instead of searching for well-balanced attacks to unsettle the West Indies' batting line-up, the opposition went around in a frenzy looking for fast bowling attacks to match it with the Windies. They overlooked one important point.

The reason for the West Indies' success was not just the four fast men, it was the quality of those bowlers. At first it was Roberts, Holding, Joel Garner and Colin Croft. That's a balance of three great bowlers and one good one. Then later it became Holding, Garner, Malcolm Marshall and either Patrick Patterson or Courtney Walsh, which did nothing to alter that balance.

India used to win their share of matches with no fast bowlers and only an average batting line-up, but with three excellent spinners in Erapali Prasanna, Bishen Bedi and Bhagwat Chandrasekar.

It's the quality of bowling that brings victories, not pace alone. Have a look at the way the West Indies have recently struggled to maintain their position of dominance. Sure, they lost a lot of batting with the retirement of Lloyd, Viv Richards and Gordon Greenidge, but as well as this, the bowling attack of Curtly Ambrose, Patterson, Walsh and an aging Marshall, while good, was nothing like when it comprised three great ones and one good one. It makes a big difference.

What has helped the West Indies cling to power is the lack of aggressive response shown by opposing batsmen. In a period of unparalleled dominance by fast bowlers, we have more front-foot players than I've ever seen before, and less batsmen employing the horizontal bat shots. How can this be?

Maybe this period, coinciding as it has with an increase in Limited-over cricket and its prohibitive restrictions on short-pitched bowling, has produced a breed of front-footers? Maybe the administrators, thinking they were helping the batsmen by putting these restrictions in place, were actually hindering them? Maybe the helmet and all the other protective equipment is making the batsmen lazy with their feet? One thing is for certain, more batsmen are hit now than before the arrival of all this armoury.

Maybe the preponderance of coaches who have suddenly appeared on the horizon, waving certificates which say they are coaches, but with very little else to recommend them, are not doing their job properly?

It's more likely to be a combination of all those things, and perhaps a few others to boot. But one thing is for sure, the fast bowlers have had the upperhand for a while now, and it's been disappointing that the batsmen haven't tried to do more to wrest the initiative. In this same period the West Indies have provided the bulk of the hookers and pullers, and precious few batsmen from other nations have shown an inclination to 'take on' the fast bowlers and in particular the short-pitched stuff.

Fast men are like any other bowlers; they don't like runs being scored off their bowling and they especially hate their figures increasing in increments of four. I don't believe you can sit back and wait for fast bowlers to get tired and hope to win many matches. In fact, I don't think you'll even hang on for a draw too often using this method. I have always believed that if a batsman is tied down, it's his duty to do something positive about it, not just to wait for the bowlers to make a mistake.

In conclusion, I would have to say that I think the bowlers have taken the upperhand in the never-ending battle with the batsmen. They have been aided and abetted in their task by a weak administration which has been glacial-like in its efforts to increase criminally slow over rates. One can't blame the bowlers in this matter, because so often have they been on the receiving end of administrative injustices, that they have probably decided to enjoy it while it lasts.

Well, to some degree the picnic is over. Unfortunately, as so often happens, the administrators have got it 'arse up with care'. They stepped in and nominated the number of short-pitched deliveries allowed per over, per batsmen, which gives far too much of an advantage to the batsmen. What they should have done is at least ensure the bowlers send down more deliveries in a day to even up the contest. That would then put the onus on the batsmen to battle their own way out of the doldrums in what would be a much fairer fight.

That is the way the never-ending battle should continue to be fought, with the game of cricket as the chief beneficiary.

Viv Richards, The Master Blaster.

Colin 'Ollie' Milburn, a great character, and, on his day, a destroyer of bowling attacks.

Barry Richards had mostly good days and I was fortunate to witness one of the best, 325 in a day for South Australia. Every inch a cricketer.

A bad sight for bowlers. Garry Sobers and Graeme Pollock,
numbers 'one' and 'two' respectively, relaxing before the SCG International
on The Rest of the World tour, 1971-72.

The best batsman and allrounder.
Garry Sobers excelled at any sport he played.

Greg Chappell. Elegance with a well organised mind.

A nightmare for batsmen, Dennis Lillee and Jeff Thomson. They were tough on Englishmen and no more gentle on team-mates, as Ashley Mallett found out in a Sheffield Shield game.

Doug Walters always argued Bishen Bedi (left) was a better bowler than Erapali Prasanna. Doug could be very convincing...here he pulls Prasanna for four.

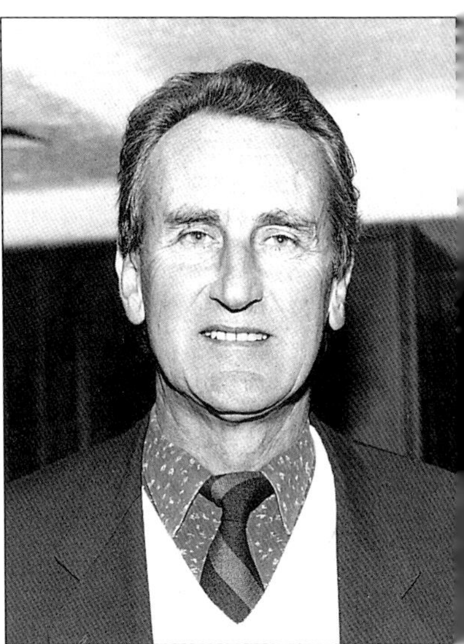

Jack Fingleton (hat) told me "Never trust a pom". He reckoned he was vindicated after the Fuserium Fiasco at Headingley in 1972.

Ted Dexter (above right) said as a captain I was a 'flashy dresser'. That is one wa of describing the fashions of 1972.

SIMPLY THE BEST

"The Captain Cocked up his Arithmetic."

"Who is the best bowler you've faced?"

That is the question I'm most often asked at a gathering of sports fans. Next in line comes, "Who is the fastest bowler?" then "Who is the best batsmen?" and so on and so forth. Well, here goes. I'll give you more bests than an Irish phone book.

The best opposition fast bowler I ever faced was John Snow, by a touch from Andy Roberts.

John Snow was fast, accurate, always learning and he hated baggy green caps.

When I mention Snow in the fast bowler bracket, the quizmaster often says, "But he wasn't really fast."

I immediately know this gentleman hasn't faced Snowball from twenty metres, particularly at the WACA or the SCG. He was quick at times, not quite in the top bracket, but in a Test match his pace didn't drop much and he always had a little room under the accelerator pedal for important moments.

When I first faced Snow in 1968, he was predominantly a cutter of the ball, with an exceptionally good leg-cutter. By the time I last faced him in 1975 he'd added swing to his armoury and also bowled a good slower ball.

He had a damned good bouncer, especially in Australia, where he didn't have to pitch the ball in as short as in England. He gave you no early warning signs when he bowled a short one, as he retained his well-balanced jog to the wicket and used just a little more shoulder to gain extra pace and bounce. His short deliveries were inevitably well-directed and often they rose sharply off quite a reasonable length.

A bouncer can be fast and it can be accurate, but if the batsman gets an early warning that it's coming, then it's far easier to handle.

Snowball was a great competitor, especially against Australia, and I think Ray Illingworth managed to extract just a little more effort from John than any other England captain.

Like most fast bowlers, Snow was a bit on the surly side and didn't have much to say in our early days of combat. However, as he got older and slowed down a little, he was more approachable and I found him to be a good bloke. I get the feeling that most young fast bowlers believe being friendly with opposition batsmen will lessen their impact on the field.

South Africa's Peter Pollock was the pace bowler who changed most noticeably in the space of two tours. In 1966-67 you were lucky if you got a grunt out of 'Big Pooch' when you said "Good morning Peter." By 1969-70 he was not only drinking with us in the dressingroom, but would occasionally socialise with us away from the cricket ground.

One night, with a few beers under my belt, I said to Peter, "You were an ignorant prick on the last tour and now you're a good bloke. What brought about the change?"

"I discovered," said Peter, "there was an opportunity to make a few good friends in this game." Then he smiled and added, "I hope I haven't left it too late."

These days Peter follows a religious path. A simple change from convincing batsmen to converting citizens.

There was nothing christian about John Snow's approach. He was out in the middle to rid the world of batsmen, especially those wearing baggy green caps. Snowy never said as much, in fact he never said a word to me on the field, but his occasional glares adequately conveyed his message.

Apart from being a fine fast bowler, John Snow was also a poet. His definition of a bouncer is a classic, delivered exactly the way he bowled them, straight to the point. He wrote, it's "a short and emphatic examination paper that you put to the batsman".

Andy Roberts is the strong silent type, but, like Snowball, he had a meaningful glare. Also like John, he had a strong right shoulder and he used it to good effect when bowling a bouncer. And like Snow, he gave no early warning signal.

There were a lot of similarities between Snow and Roberts. Both used to cut the ball more than swing it, they were about the same speed, with Roberts being a touch quicker and they were both very accurate for bowlers of their pace.

Andy was a shrewd bowler and I credit him with playing a large part in the West Indies' renaissance in the mid-seventies. It was his hard-nosed attitude, along with Viv Richards and 'keeper Deryck Murray during World Series Cricket, that helped to catapult the West Indies to the top.

Andy was a mean bowler in the best sense of the word. He had been troubling me with short lifting deliveries into the rib-cage area in the first Test in 1975-76. I was sweating on something to hook or pull so I could do a bit of terrorising of my own and whistle one past the ear of the short-leg fieldsman.

I finally got one in the perfect spot, aimed at the right shoulder. Delighted, I smashed it away to the square-leg boundary and looked forward to a few more of those. I played against Andy on a fairly regular basis until I retired in early 1980, but I never got another bouncer aimed at my right shoulder.

When I was in the Caribbean in 1991 as a commentator, I was having a drink with Andy one night after play. I asked him if he remembered the delivery at the Gabba. "Sure I do, Ian," he replied. "I never bowled you another one because you obviously liked them there."

Good fast bowlers have a memory like an elephant.

The fastest bowlers I ever faced were Jeff Thomson and Michael Holding. There may have been a slight difference in speed between the two, but it didn't allow you time to change your mind. If your first choice was wrong you had to hope your luck was in.

Apparently, the best recorded reflexes react in 0.42 of a second. According to the mathematicians, you had 0.47 of a second from the time the ball left Thommo's hand until it reached the batsman. It's no wonder many a batsman was late on the shot and many more felt the sensation of the ball hitting the bat, rather than vice-versa.

I only remember feeling that unnerving sensation once, the first time I faced Andy Roberts. It was at The Oval in 1975, during a qualifying match in the World Cup. I made a mental note to sharpen the footwork on the next delivery.

Until he busted his shoulder at the Adelaide Oval in a collision with Alan 'Fitter'n' Turner, as they both attempted to catch a skied pull shot from Zaheer Abbas, Thommo was the most lethal fast bowler I'd seen.

He made the ball climb off a good length and go past about Adam's apple height. I saw a few batsmen who faced Thommo come away with a look on their face that suggested they wished Adam and Eve had never met.

Thommo was the only fast bowler that I felt was unhookable. His bouncer usually passed by a few feet overhead and the 'climber' was never short enough to hook.

He was never quite the same after that collision in 1976. And I think Thommo had an inkling of what was to come at the time. As he lay on the ground a few feet away from Turner, he muttered, "I'll knock this bloke's (Zaheer) head off." Then he added as he grimaced in pain, "That's if I ever fuckin' bowl again."

Thommo was unique. He was a genuine speed merchant who liked nothing better than bowling fast. In Trinidad in 1979 he took five wickets in the first innings, but in the second dig on a wicket that had flattened right out it was virtually impossible to bowl him after his opening spell.

After we'd won the game by about twenty runs, I had a quiet chat with Jeff. "Why," I suggested, "don't you have a yarn with Dennis about how to cut the ball and bowl on slower tracks?"

"I know what you're saying," replied Thommo, "but if you don't mind, I'd like to do it my way."

I also understood. He was a fast bowler, and he was going to live or die on speed. When asked to describe his action,

Thommo once said, “Ahh, I just shuffle up and go wang.”

When I told this to former NSW opener Warren ‘Wacky’ Saunders, who’d been hit in the head by Thommo whilst batting for St. George, he replied, “Yeah. But he went wang pretty bloody quick.”

The best fast bowler I ever saw was Thommo’s partner in pace, Dennis Keith Lillee.

Lillee was fast, fiery and fearsome. He also had all the tools, which he kept finely tuned by training extremely hard, and he was a fast learner. On top of that, he was the most determined cricketer I’ve come across. If anyone ever mastered his bowling (which was rare), they still had to overcome his iron will.

In the second innings of The Oval Test in 1972 he was exhausted after a long tour and a lot of bowling in that match. Ashley ‘Rowdy’ Mallett had just trapped Geoff Arnold leg before and we had gathered to congratulate ‘Rowdy’ on a fine piece of bowling. Suddenly Lillee piped up, “We mustn’t let these bastards get too many more. We’re chasing 240-odd now and that’s about enough.”

Having made a succinct speech, he then made short work of Alan Knott, clean bowling him without addition to England’s total. It was an amazing performance. Lillee was dog tired, Knott was in superb form and the ball didn’t deviate, but somehow Dennis got through Knott’s usually impregnable defence with one that beat him for pace. It gave Dennis ten wickets for the match and, after a long hard battle, Australia clinched a memorable victory.

In 1979 in Trinidad, on a hot humid day when the dust from the dry ground filled your lungs everytime you tried to breathe, I’d bowled him for an extended spell as wickets were at a premium and runs precious.

I hadn’t realised how extended the spell was until I asked him how he was going. His mouth was working, but no words were coming out. He was exhausted, but he still took the ball from me and walked back to his mark. He must have bowled that last over purely on will power.

On that same tour his back gave out during the final Test in

Antigua. As the game was heading towards a draw, I told him to book his flight home the next day so he could get some treatment from his own personal doctor.

We had a farewell drink for Dennis that night, so you can imagine my surprise the next morning when I walked into the hotel lobby just as he boarded the bus for the ground.

"What the hell are you doing?" I enquired.

"Oh, my back felt better when I woke up," he smiled, "so I went for a run and then bowled a few balls to 'Doc' (our physio, Dave McErlane) and I've decided to finish out the match."

And finish it he did. With six West Indies wickets.

I never once recall hearing Dennis ask for a fieldsman to be moved into a defensive position after runs had been taken from his bowling. He was more likely to ask for the bat pad to be moved a yard closer or an extra slip to be added. Dennis was only interested in taking wickets and he was never interested in their cost.

Dennis Lillee was a captain's dream and a batsman's nightmare.

The best batsman I've ever seen was Garry (now Sir Garfield) Sobers. I'm not including all his other assets as a cricketer, this is as a batsman pure and simple. His technique was simple and his batting a pure joy to watch.

He had every shot in the book and he had the technique to bat anywhere in the order. In his first Test, Garry played as an orthodox spinner and batted number nine. In his fourth Test he opened the batting against Ray Lindwall and Keith Miller, and made 43 before he was dismissed by off-spinner Ian Johnson.

As an eighteen-year-old twelfth man for SA, I watched open-mouthed as he demolished a NSW attack including Alan Davidson and Richie Benaud, while making 251. When Benaud recalled Davidson to put the brakes on his progress, he promptly hit him for four, six, four. The six scattered the delirious patrons at the Adelaide Oval scoreboard bar.

I had the part pleasure, part painful experience of captaining an Australian team that fetched and carried while he amassed

254 for the Rest of the World XI at the MCG in 1971-72.

Lillee had got Garry for a duck in the first innings and he was keen to make amends. By stumps on the third day he was 132 not out, and over a drink in the Australian dressingroom he confided, "Ian, Prue (his wife) has left me."

"Garry," I said, mindful of the thrashing we were receiving, "if that's what is making you angry, give me her phone number. I'll talk her into returning home immediately."

After Garry had completed his demolition job (and Prue had returned home), I got a call from a mate of mine, Ray Hogan, who had played against Garry in the Leagues in Lancashire.

"Ian," he started, "you've got your field in the wrong place for Sobers."

I didn't let him get any further. "Yes, you're right Ray," I answered. "They were at the MCG. If I'd had any sense we'd have been at the SCG."

Garry's simple technique suggested a casual approach to batting. That wasn't the case. He knew exactly what he was doing and he was a very determined character.

In his last season for South Australia, we were playing against the touring South African side, and I distinctly recall Garry saying to Les Favell, "Okay if I wear the West Indies' cap today, skip?"

Les agreed to his request and on the only occasion I saw Garry bat in a cap for SA, he made 154 against South Africa. The sight of that maroon cap with the peak pointed skywards like a jockey booting home a winner always stuck in my mind.

Years later I asked Garry if there was any significance in his wearing the West Indies' cap that day. He just smiled that endearing gap-toothed grin of his and said, "No Ian. I just figured it was time the South Africans had their first look at a West Indies' cap."

Not only was Sobers a great cricketer, he was also a bloody fine bloke. I will always relish those two and a bit seasons I played with the best cricketer of my time. I appreciated the fact that he always treated me as an equal and was there to offer advice anytime I asked. There was never any suggestion that as a junior in the SA team I shouldn't be in his company socially, and I enjoyed many a chat with him over a beer.

I'm glad my parents brought me up without any prejudice when it came to judging human beings. If I ever needed any confirmation that this was the right approach, it was provided for me by Garry Sobers.

I have Garry just a touch ahead of another fine left-handed batsman, Graeme Pollock of South Africa.

Graeme was born to be a number four. I first saw him bat as a nineteen-year-old at the Adelaide Oval in 1963-64 when he pulverised the Australian attack in making a memorable 175. Two sixes in one over from Bob Simpson cleared the Eastern gate (as it was then) and bounced merrily down the road at about double the speed limit. On many occasions after that I saw him bat at four and he always looked as comfortable as a King sitting on his throne.

At Durban in 1970, Barry Richards had threatened to dethrone the King of South African batting by scoring a marvellous 94 before lunch on the first day.

Ali Bacher had been dismissed by Alan Connolly with four balls remaining in the last over before lunch. During the interval, Kingsmead was abuzz with the name Barry Richards; it was flying around the ground like a swarm of bees.

On resumption, Pollock blasted a couple of balls from Connolly's unfinished over, to the boundary. Following that outburst, he leant on his bat as if to say, "Hey, there's someone else out here besides Richards. Take note."

I certainly did. Keith Stackpole was standing next to me in the slips and I said, "Stacky, I reckon we're in trouble. This bastard's announced his arrival and now he's going to see how many Richards gets and then outscore him."

Richards made 140. Pollock was eventually c&b Stackpole for 274. That was the best Test innings I've seen played by an opponent. However, Graeme didn't limit his exploits to the longer game, and played one of the most extraordinary Limited-overs innings, against South African provincial side Border.

It was a sixty overs a side game and Graeme, as usual, came

in at number four—in the twelfth over. At the end of the innings he remained not out 222. That's right, Two-Two-Two, scored off 165 balls in the space of only 48 overs.

When I first heard the tale of 222, I thought someone was taking advantage of South Africa's isolation to perpetrate the most extravagant exaggeration known to man. When I next ran into Graeme he confirmed that he had indeed made 222 not out in a Limited-overs match. When I asked how he did it, he replied, "Ahh, the opposition captain cocked up his arithmetic."

"In what way?" I continued the interrogation.

"Well," G.P. laughed, "he finished up with a couple of non-bowlers and I made seventy-four off the last four overs."

I don't care if it's the Gulargambone thirds bowling, there are very few batsman who could demolish an attack the way Graeme Pollock could.

I place Sobers ahead of Pollock purely because Garry was a fabulous hooker and Graeme didn't indulge.

If you want someone to march to the wicket and immediately proceed to tear an attack apart, Viv Richards is the man I'd choose for the job.

His 153 not out off just 130 balls at the MCG in 1979-80 was a masterpiece. It was played in a World Series Cup match against an Australian attack which included Dennis Lillee, Jeff Thomson and Rodney Hogg. His lone six tore into the fourth row of the wooden seats just near the Member's stand sightboard, like a doodlebug on the loose. If the spectators hadn't been watching closely, it would have been just as dangerous.

For the batsman with the best organised mind while at the crease, I'd plump for brother Greg.

I found out at a very young age how determined Greg could be during our backyard 'Tests'. Despite being saddled with the burden of 'representing' England, he was always difficult to dismiss. Possessing a well-organised mind at a young age, he had an immediate answer every time I asked him, "Why wasn't that out?"

He displayed all his powers of concentration and

determination in his 132 at Lord's in 1972. That innings is often overlooked in its importance to the team, because it coincided with Bob Massie's incredible debut figures of 16/137.

Near the end of his career, Greg complained that he wasn't able to dredge up all his concentration as often as he would like. But, typically, he announced his retirement before the last Test against Pakistan in 1983-84, while still needing sixty-nine runs to pass Sir Donald Bradman's Australian record.

Having set himself a task, he summoned all his powers of concentration for one last supreme effort. He finished with 182 and concluded his glittering Test career just as he'd started it—with a century.

I mentioned Graeme Pollock's 222 not out in a Gillette Cup match in South Africa. Unfortunately, I didn't witness that innings. There are three other innings I wish I'd seen.

The first one was Englishman Colin 'Ollie' Milburn's 243 for WA against Queensland at the Gabba. He made them in two sessions, with 180 coming off his own bat in the two hours between lunch and tea.

At lunch on a typically hot, humid day at the Gabba, Ollie gulped down fluid, then remarked to a soul mate in thirst, Rod Marsh, "Blooody hell Rodney it's 'ot. I woont be roonin' too many after loonch."

As good as his word, Ollie smashed the bowling to all parts of the field and, in the opinion of Marsh, "every shot had the power to go to the boundary, it was just that a few of them were stopped."

Kapil Dev's 175 in the 1983 World Cup against Zimbabwe is another sight I'm sorry to have missed. Coming in at 5/17 Kapil, who was captain of India at the time, launched a mortar attack which bombarded the bowlers to the tune of six sixes and seventeen fours.

Not surprisingly, it was a match-winning innings, but as it turned out, it could well have been a World Cup winning dig. In a boilover, India beat the West Indies in the final by 43 runs, but without that win over Zimbabwe they would have struggled to qualify for the semi-finals.

Viv Richards' 189 not out at Old Trafford in a Limited-overs game against England in 1984 had similar qualities to Kapil's incredible innings. Scored off only 170 balls, it included five sixes and twenty-one fours and in an unfinished tenth wicket partnership with Michael Holding, added 106. Holding remained not out 12.

Viv's best is always worth seeing.

Fortunately I did see Barry Richards' best. He made 325 in a day for South Australia against WA at the WACA ground in 1970-71. At that time a Shield day comprised three hundred and thirty minutes' play. The WA attack included Graham McKenzie, Dennis Lillee, Tony Lock and Tony Mann. All four bowlers played Test cricket, with Lillee taking 355 wickets, McKenzie 246 and Lock 174.

It was the season before bonus points came in and we worked out that SA would have received fourteen batting bonus points that day with the stumps score being 3/513.

At one stage it looked like Barry was going to fall just short of three hundred and finish with something like 280. However, he moved into another gear (it had to be overdrive) and I can vividly recall the finish of the day. He belted Lillee off the back foot straight down the ground and before the ball had hit the sight-board on the second bounce, Barry had the gloves off and was heading for the pavilion, as if to say, "Well, that concludes another day's work."

On the same ground about four years later, Doug Walters scored one of his three hundreds in a session in Test cricket. The others were made in Trinidad and during his 250 at Lancaster Park, Christchurch. Incidentally, he also scored a century in a session against the Rest of the World XI at the MCG in 1971-72.

The records on centuries in a session are a little clouded but, apart from Sir Donald Bradman, I can't find any player with more than Dashing Doug.

His innings at Queen's Park Oval in Trinidad could well have set the wheels in motion for his feat at the WACA ground. In 1973, West Indies off-spinner Lance Gibbs dismissed Greg

Chappell with the second ball of the last over before lunch. After dealing with his curried goat, Doug proceeded to make mincemeat of the West Indies attack. He signalled his intentions by cover driving the first ball he received on resumption to the boundary.

This was a sign that something special was about to occur, because I believe the cover drive against an off-spinner on a pitch that's taking turn is one of the most difficult in the game.

At one stage Gibbs had a six (on-side), three field. Doug belted a ball over mid-wicket, one bounce into the advertising hoardings, so Gibbs took the man from point and placed him on the mid-wicket boundary. It was now a seven, two field.

The next ball pitched in almost the identical spot and Doug backed away and cut it past point to the boundary. The frustrated bowler waved the man from mid-wicket back to point. He then pitched one in a similar spot and Doug repeated the first boundary shot. Gibbs shrugged his shoulders, threw up his hands and walked away a disillusioned man.

Doug went from 0 to 102 in that session, in the finest innings I've seen on a pitch taking a lot of turn.

About twenty-one months later at the WACA ground, Greg was dismissed by Bob Willis with just a few minutes remaining before tea. As Greg passed Doug on his way to the wicket, he simply said, "This time I've given you a bit of a sighter."

Doug was 3 not out at tea. Nothing more was said, although Greg had made a few of us aware of his earlier comment.

At drinks, with Doug well into his sixties, I said to twelfth man Terry Jenner, "Check with the little fella and see what his chances are."

As Terry handed Doug a drink, he asked, "How's it going?"

Doug's typically laconic reply was, "Oh, it's a bit warm."

"Not the weather," scolded Terry, "how's *it* going?"

"I think I've got a chance," was his reply.

That was the extent of the conversation; at no time was a century in a session mentioned. Nevertheless, when it came to the last over of the day, Bob Willis bowling and Doug needing ten for a hundred in a session, we were all betting he'd do it.

Even when it came to the last ball and he still needed six, most people in the dressingroom said, "Somehow the little bastard will find a way."

And he did. With a magnificent pull shot over the mid-wicket boundary rope.

Doug Walters is certainly the most incredible cricketer I've ever played with or against. Unfortunately, I think they might have broken the mould when Doug was born, which is a pity, because everybody should have the pleasure of playing with a Doug Walters type—they tend to keep the game in perspective.

Doug and I had our occasional disagreement, and it was usually over the question of who was the best spin bowler we'd ever played against. Doug said Bishen Bedi and I plumped for Erapalli Prasanna, both of India.

I thought Pras was a genius. He had beautiful flight with his off-the-shoulder style action. So many times when the ball left his hand, it appeared to be an invitation to a juicy half-volley, but it never kept the appointment. I used to wonder if Pras had the ball on a string, which he tugged just as you were about to play the shot.

Pras was equally adept at spinning a web of confusion on both the hard Australian pitches and on the more receptive surfaces in India.

Ashley Mallett was the best spinner I played with and he could similarly bamboozle batsmen with his flight. The main difference between Rowdy and Prasanna was that the Australian curved the ball away from the right-hand batsman more, while the much shorter Indian tended to drop it on you with his over-spin.

Ashley was known as 'Rowdy' for his quiet demeanour, but underneath that exterior smouldered a very determined off-spinner. He would get very angry if he thought a batsman was having any good fortune, but he would keep it to himself, apart from occasionally snatching his cap from the umpire.

Rowdy had a big heart and the better the batsman he was facing, the better he would bowl. When he was playing for Queensland, I once saw Greg take to Rowdy and hit eighteen off an over in an attempt to belt him out of the attack. The next three overs from Mallett were the best I've seen from a spinner. Not only didn't Greg score a run, he had to fight every inch of the way just to survive. It was a brilliant contest to watch from first slip.

In 1974-75 the Australian selectors left Mallett out of the first Test in Brisbane. When I queried Sam Loxton on why Mallett was missing, he replied in his theatrical manner, "Ooohh, he's bowling too many bad balllllls. Full tosses and loooong hops."

"That's strange," I said, "I haven't seen too many gifts, and I've been fielding at first slip all summer." After discussing the matter further, I asked for Mallet to be reinstated, because, as I argued, "If this series gets tight then I want Mallett. He won't let Australia down."

Mallett was selected for the next Test and duly had the honour of picking up the wicket (at the SCG) which resulted in Australia regaining the Ashes.

The most difficult spinner to score off was England's 'Deadly' Derek Underwood. Deadly was difficult for a right-hander because he was too quick through the air to regularly use your feet and because he didn't try to spin them all, rather angle the ball in at you from around the wicket. His line and length was impeccable and you didn't get much to cut.

On a dampish pitch he was a nightmare. He'd give you absolutely nothing to score off and then the odd one would take off like Superman—up, up and away.

I remember one he bowled to Doug Walters on the Fuserium pitch at Headingley in 1972. It climbed straight over the shoulder of Doug's bat and Alan Knott took it beside his right ear. What a combination they were—Underwood and Knott.

Knotty was the best 'keeper I saw, just a smidgeon ahead of Rodney William Marsh, purely on his ability standing up to Underwood. On that score Marsh was handicapped a little, because the English combination also played together for Kent. Marsh, on the other hand, played a lot on the bouncy WACA pitch and didn't have the luxury of seeing much spin. Apart from a period when Bruce Yardley was in the Australian side, Rod was always 'keeping in a Test to a spinner from another State side.

Both Knott and Marsh were brilliant standing back, agile and never afraid to throw themselves for a wide edge. Australia made better use of Marsh's agility, with a bigger gap between 'keeper and first slip than the Englishmen. This has the advantage of giving the slips cordon a wider arc.

So often in Ashes Tests, Knott and Marsh used to cancel each other out with their batting. Both players had the happy knack of making runs when their team needed them most.

Being the wicket-keeper's friend, I provided Knott with countless dismissals, but I did get something from him in return. Following the announcement of World Series Cricket, I was having trouble convincing Kerry Packer he should sign Ashley Mallett to a contract. "Bloody straight-breaker," growled Kerry, "wouldn't get me out."

We'd come to an agreement that if Mallett could dismiss Kerry in an over (8 ball), he'd sign the lanky off-spinner. Just before the fourth Test at Headingley in 1977 we'd been unable to arrange this contest and Mallett was still unsigned.

Kerry Packer had invited the English WSC signatories to dinner and I grabbed my opportunity. "Kerry," I piped up during a lull in conversation, "ask Alan Knott what he thinks of Mallett's bowling."

"You've set this up," he bellowed, glaring in Alan's direction.

Despite this intimidation, which was the equal of anything he'd experienced when facing Dennis Lillee, Knotty, in his softly spoken manner, came through: "Best spinner from Australia by far."

Mallett was duly signed, but to this day I haven't been able to convince Packer that Rowdy can bowl. Mind you, Kerry hasn't yet faced him in the nets either.

Kerry bought three cricket teams during World Series Cricket: The Australians, the West Indies and a World team. If I could buy two I'd put on a special match at the MCG.

It would be between a team of compulsive hookers and a

team of bowlers who always liked to know how much bounce was in the pitch. As an added attraction, I would fly out forty thousand fans from the Caribbean to attend the match.

I reckon the contest would be worth seeing and the comments worth hearing. The teams, with my reasons for selection, are as follows.

BATTING			BOWLING	
Keith Stackpole	Aus		Uton Dowe	WI
Cammie Smith	WI		Len Pascoe	Aus
Les Favell	Aus		Des Hoare	Aus
Colin Milburn	Eng		Colin Croft	WI
Viv Richards	WI		Dennis Lillee	Aus
Garry Sobers	WI		Sarfraz Nawaz	Pak
Ali Bacher	SAf		Peter Pollock	SAf
Peter Burge	Aus		Fred Trueman	Eng
Denis Lindsay	SAf		Imran Khan	Pak
Richie Benaud	Aus		Charlie Griffith	WI
Jeff Thomson	Aus		Dave Renneberg	Aus
Eric Freeman	Aus	*12th*	John 'JK' Holt jun.	WI

BATSMEN:

Keith Stackpole: A good hooker. Once smashed Uton Dowe's bouncers to all sections of Sabina Park. When skipper Rohan Kanhai called on Uton for a second spell, a wag in the crowd yelled out, "Kanhai. You not heard de eleventh commandment. Dowe shall not bowl."

Cammie Smith: The original happy hooker. Cammie, wearing his permanent grin, once hooked the first ball of the innings for six against NSW. Would be the perfect opening partner for Stacky, whose nickname was 'Grumpy'.

Les Favell: Only man I know of who baited fast bowlers so they'd pitch the ball short. Great hooker and cutter. He once top-edged a hook shot off Wes Hall that parted his hair. When he nonchalantly hooked the next ball for four, Garry Sobers was heard to mutter, "This man is mad. He has no fear."

Colin 'Ollie' Milburn: Any man who can score 180 off his own bat in a session must be in the side for entertainment value alone. However, Ollie was no slouch when the bouncers were flying and once cut a ball for six at the WACA.

Viv Richards: Impossible to intimidate. When he heard umpire Max O'Connell tell Len Pascoe, "No more bouncers this over," Viv piped up, "Don't stop him Max."

Garry Sobers: The best hooker I've seen. In 1960-61, an enraged fast bowler at the WACA made the mistake of calling Garry 'A black so and so'. Garry's retort was to tell the (genuine) fast bowler, "Son, you're not quick enough to bowl short." Predictably, the next ball was a bouncer which Garry despatched to the fence *in front of square leg.*

Ali Bacher: Dealing with the ANC and the complexities of International cricket administration would've been a breeze for a man with Ali's batting philosophy. He believed that everything short of a half-volley was hookable.

Peter Burge: Only batsman I know who took block and then called out to the bowler, "Right." His eagerness to attack the bowling resulted in an Eastern gate appearing at Adelaide Oval. Burgey's pull shots knocked out so many pickets they decided it was easier to make a gate.

Denis Lindsay: Wicket-keeper who scored 606 runs in the series against Australia in 1966-67. 602 came from hook and pull shots. Dave Renneberg hit him in the head with a bouncer in the second Test and never stopped trying to repeat the dose.

Richie Benaud: In his initial first-class season Richie was carried off the ground with a fractured skull after missing an attempted hook shot. Fifteen years later he retired as a compulsive hooker.

Jeff Thomson: In 1975 Northamptonshire medium-fast bowler Sarfraz Nawaz told the press, "I've checked with the local cemetery and they have one coffin left. I told the guy to put Jeff Thomson's name on it." Thommo was out, attempting to hook Sarfraz in that match.

Eric Freeman (12th): I'm not sure how Fritzy hooked but we'd find out if someone got injured. He bounced out Charlie Griffith once and before the angry quick departed the scene, he enquired of wicket-keeper Barry Jarman, "What number dat man bat?"

BOWLERS:

Uton Dowe: His opening barrage of short ones to Stacky would get the game off to a perfect start. His Sabina Park cheer squad would also help make the Caribbean contingent feel at home.

Len Pascoe: Not a renowned swinger of the ball. When we were leaving St. Lucia in 1979 after a washout, Rod Marsh pleaded with the bus driver to turn back. "Lennie won't be able to sleep tonight," explained Rod, "not knowing whether this pitch had any bounce in it."

Des Hoare: Once hit South Australian number nine batsman David 'Evildick' Sincock behind the ear with his fourth successive bouncer. When he joined David for a drink after play, Des examined the wound and remarked, "Cut yourself shaving, Evil?"

Colin Croft: Once pitched one up in New Zealand in 1980, but later explained that his hand had clipped the umpire's head in delivering the ball. Crofty used to continually bowl short, working on the theory that three might be wasted, but the other three could be rip snorters.

Dennis Lillee: In a reflective mood, Dennis is sorry for every bouncer he ever bowled. Does a lot of apologising over a drink.

Sarfraz Nawaz: Only fast bowler crazy enough to bounce Thommo, *before* Jeffrey seriously injured his shoulder.

Peter Pollock: One of the few fast bowlers who "was equally adept at playing 'em or bowling 'em". Used to play bouncers with a straight bat and laugh. Great company for Cammie Smith.

Fred Trueman: Claims he didn't have to bowl bouncers to take wickets. That makes him the only fast bowler who bowled them for fun. Fred would provide the humour when someone dropped a catch at fine leg off his bowling.

Imran Khan: Imran once confided that he didn't swing the ball much. When I replied, "Imran, it usually doesn't swing when it lands only ten feet from your hand," he had a hurt look on his face.

Charlie Griffith: For variety he used to bowl a very good yorker. He was in the Australian XI dressingroom at the WACA when Wes Hall hit Tony Lock in the neck with a bouncer. Charlie fell off his chair laughing.

Dave Renneberg: Big Shine was very accurate at drawing crosses on his forehead. However, direct hits from twenty metres were rare. Dave strictly adhered to the fast bowlers' adage that you "have a few beers at night so you had the strength to bang 'em in short the next day".

John 'JK' Holt jun. (12th): On the day prior to former West Indies Test cricketer Leslie Hylton being hanged for murder, JK dropped four catches at fine leg. The next day a sign appeared at Kensington Oval, Barbados, which read, "Hang Holt, Save Hylton." He'd be the perfect fine leg for Fiery Fred.

That is only a dream match, but in the real world of International cricket it's runs and wickets that count. I also happen to believe that it's when you get them that really counts and that has come into my calculations in nominating those who I think are simply The Best.

YE OLDE ENEMY

"Never Trust the Poms."

It was at the Somerset County Ground in Taunton that I got a message to visit Jack Fingleton in the press box. It was during the 1968 tour and he caught me at a good moment—I'd just compiled a confidence-building century after making a slow start to the tour.

As I walked up the stairs I imagined the reason for Fingo's call was to congratulate me on my innings. He was a great mate of my grandfather's and I'm sure Vic would have told Jack to keep a fatherly eye on me during the tour.

However, it turned out he had much more important things on his mind.

After a polite "congratulations", he said, "This brother of yours can play a bit, can't he?" Greg, who was having the first of two seasons with Somerset, had just made fifty against the Australians.

"Yes," I joked, "I taught him well in the backyard games."

Unfazed by my flippancy Jack continued, "I've seen him play a few Shield innings," he said, "but watching him bat against (Graham) McKenzie I realised he's better than I first thought. He could go a long way."

Surprised, but delighted that Jack felt that way about Greg, I was about to take my leave, when he tapped my arm. "Just one more thing," confided Jack. "Never trust the poms."

With that Fingo turned to his typewriter and I knew it was time to leave.

I've thought about that statement many times. It confirmed a suspicion that had been lurking in my mind since I was a boy.

Reflecting on Jack's comment, I didn't think for a minute that he meant this distrust to be general. I knew he was very fond of England and had many good mates there. In fact, it was Jack who was responsible for encouraging Harold Larwood to emigrate to Australia. After some thought, I took Jack's comment to refer specifically to cricket. Over the years, I was able to narrow it down a little further.

I think the original seed of doubt was planted in my mind around about 1956. As a cricket-mad kid I used to listen to the radio through the night when Australia were playing in England. It was that year that I first went to watch Vic, who was working on a variety show on radio 5AD that was built around the cricket. Rickety Kate was the 'star' of the show and every time a wicket fell her big red nose would light up, a bell would ring and the audience would break into song. This meant a wicket had fallen in the Test match. It was much more fun when England were batting.

Unfortunately, in 1956 Kate's nose was red almost as often as the Australian batsmen's faces, during the Old Trafford Test. That was the famous game when Jim Laker took his nineteen wickets and Australia were crushed by an innings and 170 runs. Incidentally, when Jim arrived home after that match, his Austrian wife, who knew little about cricket, greeted him with, "Have you done something good, Jim? The phone has been ringing all day."

As a kid I was distraught at this loss, but as I started to climb the cricketing ladder, I heard a few stories filtering through about the pitch for that Test.

Ironically, in 1963 when I played for Ramsbottom in the Lancashire league, I was invited to play in a match for Lancashire against Cambridge University. As so often happens when cricket is played at Old Trafford, it rained for most of the match. While I was sitting around in the dressingroom, a bloke in civvies walked in and, in a heavy North of England accent, started chatting with a few of the Lancashire players.

"Who's that guy?" I enquired. "It's Bert Flack," came the answer, "the head groundsman at Old Trafford."

I immediately recognised the name as being that of the man who prepared the pitch for the 1956 Test. So I thought it was about time I found out for myself what 'that pitch' was really like from the man who prepared it.

I waited until Bert was not engaged in conversation, and said, "Excuse me, Mr. Flack. What sort of pitch did you prepare for the Test at Old Trafford in 1956?"

"'T were a bluudy bad 'un," laughed Bert, without the slightest hint of secrecy. "Them's what gives t' orders at 'eadquarters, told me t' prepare a bleedin' turner," he continued. Then he tossed his head back and burst out laughing, "And a bleedin' turner 't were."

This straightforward honesty immediately endeared me to Bert Flack and every time after that when I played at Old Trafford, I made a point of having a pint with him.

Bert never changes. He's as honest as the day is long, always speaks his mind, has a great deal of pride in his work and is extremely wary of authority.

In 1989 I was having a drink with the president of the Lancashire County Cricket Club Bob Bennett, whom I'd played against "in t' League". We were discussing Bert when, lo and behold, who should appear but the former groundsman himself.

"This old bastard," said Bob, "locked my car in the car park at Old Trafford one night after a game." (Once a car is locked in at Old Trafford it's there for the night, because the surrounding walls are about eight feet high).

"Aye that's reet," acknowledged Bert, "yooong uns were havin' a fine time, didn't give a booger about me havin' to get oop early in t' mornin'," he growled. "But, I bluudy fixed 'im," he chuckled, "he coom knockin' on t' door of 'ouse and asked, can I git car out o' car park?" recalled Bert. "And I said, 'Not unless it's got bluudy wings.'"

With tears of laughter in his eyes, Bob added, "To make matters worse, he slammed the door in my face and I had to catch a cab home."

Bert Flack was always one to give you a straight answer and when, in the Old Trafford dressingroom, he told me, "Them's what gives t' orders at 'eadquarters," I think he was unwittingly providing a clue to the meaning of Jack Fingleton's comment in 1968. I'm sure Jack had in mind some English cricket administrators when he said, "Never trust the poms."

Four years later, in 1972, Jack was livid about the pitch that was presented for the fourth Test at Headingley.

Following closely on the heels of Dennis Lillee and Bob Massie's success in the second and third Tests of that series, the fourth was played on a sparsely grassed patch of turf that resembled plasticine. It wobbled like a jelly on a plate when you prodded it with your fingers.

While we were practising on the day before the Test, vice-captain Keith Stackpole called me over and suggested we go have a look at the pitch. "You know I never look at a pitch until the morning of the game," I reminded Stacky.

"I think you'd better make an exception this time," chuckled Stackpole, "otherwise we'll go into the game with a badly balanced side."

When we reached the middle, Keith threw a ball firmly onto the pitch. It bounced no higher than the toe of his boot. He was right—it was time to re-think the composition of our side.

The official story was that the Test pitch had been infected by a fungus called Fuserium. Fuserium Oxysporum, to use it's full name, which apparently thrives in temperatures above seventy-five degrees Fahrenheit. Occurring in the chilly confines of Headingley, that in itself was enough to make me highly suspicious.

To add to the intrigue, it was the first time Derek Underwood was chosen in the England team for that series. He was nigh on unplayable under those conditions, while in the previous two Tests Lillee and Massie had claimed thirty-one of the thirty-four English wickets which had fallen.

There was a huge scream from the Australian media, and in particular, Jack Fingleton. But, to the credit of the team and at the request of the manager Ray Steele, there was no bleating from the Australian team.

That's exactly the way it should be. An International cricket team should be able to adjust to any conditions provided. That's why selectors try to choose a balanced touring party.

It was a good lesson for an emerging Australian team. It made us more determined to win the last Test (which we did) to level the series. It also taught us to be on our mettle when we were overseas, and I think it probably helped me to be well prepared for the third Test in the West Indies in 1972-73.

During the second Test in that series in Barbados, I remarked to Rod Marsh, "Something strange is going on here."

We'd played one and half Tests and the West Indies hadn't shown any inclination to push for victory. I'd heard a lot about the Queen's Park Oval pitch (where we were due to play the third and fifth Tests); from all reports it was receptive to spin.

Quite a few fans in the Caribbean had told me that without Ashley Mallett (unavailable for the tour), the West Indies were stronger than Australia when it came to spin bowling.

Putting two and two together and coming up with six (that's the sort of arithmetic you need as captain) I concluded my on-field conversation with Rodney by saying, "This mob think they can beat us in Trinidad and they're just playing a holding game until we get there."

I wasn't unhappy about the contest boiling down to the game in Trinidad and indeed it turned out to be what the West Indies had in mind. We had some very good players of spin bowling, who in my opinion were superior to our opponents, and I felt confident we'd at least give our bowlers some runs to work with.

As it turned out we made just enough, winning by forty-four runs in one of the best Tests I've played in.

Jack Fingleton's advice could just as easily have been, "Be a little suspicious of all opposition when you're playing overseas." Ain't that the truth, as I discovered before the fourth Test in Guyana.

We played a four day game against Guyana at the Bourda ground, leading up to the Test. Umpiring in that match were C.F. Vyfhuis, known to the Australian team as 'The Viper', and Cecil Kippins. Cecil, who had been umpiring Test cricket since the late fifties and used to wear a pith helmet, apparently because he'd been hit in the back of the head by a throw from a fielder, was a well-respected umpire and did a reasonable job in the tour match. On the other hand, some of our guys had reservations about Vyfhuis.

Anyway, when former West Indies player Joe Solomon called Bill Jacobs (our manager) and myself to a meeting before the Test, my highly-developed sense of suspicion was working overtime.

Fortunately, I also went into this meeting armed with the knowledge that Bill Jacobs (who was not a Board member) had told me he would back me to the hilt on any matters I thought were important to the team. I knew what that meant. Bill, who can make 'good morning' sound like a death threat, is a good man to have on your side.

No sooner had we sat down in the beautifully comfortable wicker chairs on the verandah of the old Georgetown Cricket Club pavilion, than Joe informed us the umpires for the Test would be Kippins and Vyfhuis. I immediately thought, "Uh oh, we're being set up."

We were one up in the series with two to play, one of which was back at Queen's Park Oval, where the West Indies fancied their chances of victory. I wasn't about to surrender this hard won advantage easily. Up to that point in the series the extremely competent and experienced Douglas Sang Hue had umpired in all three games. I was more than happy with his performance. He had stood with Ralph Gosein in two Tests and the highly experienced Cortez Jordan in Barbados.

I didn't feel this was the time to suddenly introduce two different umpires into the series, and I made this clear when I told Joe, "I would like Douglas (Sang Hue) and Cortez Jordan as first choice. If you feel it's necessary to have a local umpire, then I'll take Douglas and Cecil Kippins. As a last option, I'll take Douglas and anyone."

As you can see, the common thread was Sang Hue, who I thought would ensure a good standard of umpiring. Joe had different ideas. "No umpire has ever done all five Tests in the

Caribbean," he informed us, "and we think it's time to blood another umpire."

I knew he couldn't be talking about Cecil, because he'd started umpiring against Pakistan back in 1957-58. So he had to be talking about Vyfhuis, who was the main cause of my concern. "If you want to blood umpires, Joe," I replied, "you should do it early in the series, not when it's on the line."

This didn't make much of an impression on Joe, who repeated that the two locals would be in charge of the Test.

It was time to make myself clear. "In that case, Joe," I said, "I'll be the only Australian player at the ground on the first morning, and I'll only be there long enough to hear you explain to the full-house crowd the reason why only one team has turned up for play."

Joe looked more than a little stunned. His condition deteriorated when Bill Jacobs added, "And Ian has the full backing of management on this matter, Joe."

It is now history that Australia, in stunning fashion, went on to win the Test by ten wickets after trailing by twenty-five runs on the first innings. The match was umpired by Douglas Sang Hue and Cecil Kippins. Following the completion of the fifth Test in Trinidad (which Sang Hue also umpired), I told a gathering, "Douglas Sang Hue is one of the top three umpires I have played under, along with Colin Egar of Australia and Charlie Elliott of England."

Incidentally, I recently checked to see if a precedent had been set for an umpire standing in all Tests of a series in the Caribbean. I discovered that in the first series ever played there, between West Indies and England in 1929-30, J. Hardstaff sen. umpired in the four Tests played. This is also a precedent for using an umpire from each of the countries playing in the series (which I think is a preferable option to an international panel), as the J. Hardstaff sen. is the same Joe Hardstaff who played for England and later became a well-respected Test umpire.

Now, to return to that third Test in Trinidad and the reason for my confidence that Australia would have an equal chance of winning on a pitch which assisted spinners right from the start.

I was always confident our side could make 350 under any conditions (except against Underwood at Headingley in 1972), and consequently I was happy we'd be competitive in most matches anywhere in the cricket world.

With that number of runs and a bowling attack of Lillee, Thomson, Max Walker and Ashley Mallett, you're not going to lose often. Although there were many times during my captaincy period when Australia didn't have that attack, or anything like it, we were still able to win more often than the opposition. This was because the batsmen were able to give the bowlers something to work with and, just as importantly, score runs quickly enough to give the bowlers time to take twenty wickets. Since 1976-77 Australia's record overseas is abysmal. I believe a lot of the problems stem from not having players (especially batsmen) who can adapt to a variety of conditions.

For instance, the scream that went up in Pakistan in 1988, when Australia accused the opposition of preparing a sub-standard pitch, was ludicrous. The only way a home team can afford to prepare a pitch to suit themselves is when they think the opposition are vulnerable against a certain type of bowling.

Otherwise they are leaving themselves wide open. What if Pakistan had lost the toss and Australia batted first and made a big score? Then the home side would have faced the daunting prospect of batting second and fourth on a deteriorating pitch.

If Pakistan did prepare a pitch that was receptive to spin and took the odds on winning the toss, then they must have felt very confident of Australia's inability to bat well on it. If that's the case, then Australia were 'fair game'.

The only time I felt our strong batting line-up was threatened was in England, and that worry revolved around one playing condition.

On every tour I played in England (1968, 1972 and 1975) the Test pitches were never fully covered until play was called off for the day. In the case of a rain delay, the bowlers' run-ups would be covered, but not the pitch itself. What a perfect situation for Derek Underwood.

Apart from Underwood, I was also fearful of this situation

occurring because the English players were used to uncovered pitches in their County competition. However, the playing condition eventually backfired and England skipper Mike Denness lost his job in the aftermath.

The first morning of the opening Test in 1975 at Edgbaston was overcast and gloomy. It looked like it was raining everywhere but at the cricket ground, and before the toss England captain Mike Denness had several confidential meetings separately, with his bowlers and batsmen. The only thing that pleased me about that was Denness' desire to hold the meetings on the field where everyone could see them. I thought that was a sign he was trying to make a decision to please, rather than making the one that he felt was right to give England the best chance of winning the match. I needed something positive to take my mind off the thought of rain and Underwood, combining to sink Australia.

Despite my fears, I was going to bat if I won the toss, because the pitch looked good and I couldn't send the opposition in to bat in the hope that it might rain. I didn't have to worry, as Mike won the toss and inserted us.

Australia made 359 without being hindered by a drop of rain, but after one over of England's innings, down she came. By the bucketload.

If that wasn't enough to make my day, another playing condition had been added for that tour. If more than an hour's play was lost up until 6.30 (finishing time), play could continue for an extra hour.

So we had the joyous situation (for Australia) of losing more than an hour's play, then watching as Lillee, Thomson and Walker rushed up on dry run-ups and pounded the ball onto a slowly drying pitch. To add to our unbridled joy, the last hour of play, between 6.30 and 7.30 as England followed on, was played in brilliant sunshine.

With this hugely lopsided advantage, Australia went on to win the Test early on the fourth day, by an innings and eighty-five runs. The celebration on that occasion had an extra tinge of pleasure about it and late that evening in the Australian

Trade Commission tent, Rod Marsh, Rohan Kanhai and myself toasted the success of Australia.

An interesting trio, especially as Rohan had captained the West Indies in 1973 when we defeated them in the Caribbean. However, it turned out that Rohan (who was playing with Warwickshire) was just as happy as we were over the Australian victory because, like me, he was wary of the playing condition which had contributed so greatly to our victory.

It was with no great surprise, but a good deal of satisfaction, that I read about that playing condition being deleted from the English tour conditions shortly afterwards.

On occasions, I'm sure the cricket writers feel they are helping to give 'their' team a bit of an advantage in a series. Despite the unwritten rule of 'No cheering in the press box', it isn't always strictly impartial in that enclosure.

Ted Dexter, former England captain, former cricket writer and now the man charged with the responsibility of overseeing English cricket, is one who contributed in this area.

Before the Australian team left for England in 1972, Ted wrote that we were "the worst team to leave Australia's shores". He then added that I was tactically unaware and as a captain was basically just a flashy dresser.

Some time after our success at Lord's, when Massie took sixteen wickets, Ted wrote that the reason the Australians were able to swing the ball more than the Englishmen was due to 'lip ice'. He suggested we were using it on the ball more often than we used it to relieve chapped lips.

This was a load of baloney. As I've already explained, I don't condone cheating and that is what Ted was accusing us of. Even if I didn't think that way, as a batsman I would have left myself with a huge dilemma. If I knew Lillee and Massie were using some 'extraneous substance' on the ball to improve their performance, what then would I have done when SA played WA in a Shield match? Let them continue on their merry way, or scream blue murder?

If you look up the newspapers of the time you'll see I didn't scream blue murder, and I think by now you've gathered I'm not the sort of person to willingly allow the opposition any advantage.

Actually, Ted's article provided a fair amount of mirth in the Australian camp and caused umpire Eddie Phillipson a moment of embarrassment.

Ted's article appeared under blazing headlines in a Sunday paper. The next day we were continuing a County match in which Eddie was standing. I'd run down to meet Bob Massie on his way up to bowl the next over and after a brief chat I delivered his cap to Eddie.

As I was continuing my journey to first slip, Eddie jokingly asked, "Where's the lip ice, Ian?"

I always carry a small tube of lip salve. Have done so for as long as I can remember and still do. It's always in my pants pocket and I used to carry it in the fob pocket of my cricket creams.

Following Eddie's jocular comment I stopped, dug into my pocket and said, "Right here Eddie," and threw the tube to him.

Being a former County cricketer Eddie caught it easily and then took a closer look. His mood suddenly changed. "Christ," he said, as he tossed the tube into the air and well away from himself, "I don't want to see that, Ian."

I burst out laughing, picked up my lip salve and trotted back to first slip. I think I'd convinced Eddie that we weren't guilty. I'm sure he realised a guilty man wouldn't have parted with the evidence as easily as that.

Ted's next essay into the unknown came in 1977. This time he accused fast bowler Len Pascoe of being a chucker. Once again this proved to be a good source of humour among the Australian team, with captain Greg Chappell laughing it off by saying, "Hasn't he watched Len throw the ball in from the boundary? If he had, he would know as a chucker Lennie would be an inaccurate medium pacer."

Although Ted's now out of cricket writing, the tradition is being continued. When the Australian youth team were touring England recently and had a good win in the 'Test', one writer said the victory was due not so much to the ability of their leading bowler Michael Kasprowicz to move the ball, but rather his proficiency in picking the seam.

I'm sure that England players could quote numerous examples where Australian cricket writers have tried to get 'involved' in the series by writing similar articles designed to stir the pot. This tends to support the theory of Sir Robert Menzies who said, many years ago, "Great Britain and Australia are of the same blood and allegiance and history and instinctive mental processes. We know each other so well that, thank heavens, we don't have to be too tactful with each other."

The advice from Jack Fingleton was helpful, as it kept me always on the lookout for devious plots while I was Australian captain. I worked on the basis that I was suspicious of the opposition until they proved that they could be trusted. Apparently it's a comment trait with Australians.

A well-read friend of mine, Jim Kernaghan, recently pointed out a letter written to the editor of the *Sydney Morning Herald*. It appeared during the height of the storm over Prime Minister Keating's republican remarks during the Queen's tour of Australia.

The writer said he was reminded of the day he asked his father what was meant by the saying, "The sun never sets on the British Empire?"

His father replied, "Son, even God wouldn't trust the poms in the dark."

The best fast bowler I've seen, Dennis Lillee, watched over by Dickie Bird, a good umpire with a great attitude for the job.

Andy Roberts was fast, accurate, intelligent and mean as a bowler.
He taught Michael Holding (right) a lot about how to bowl.
Michael already knew how to bowl fast.

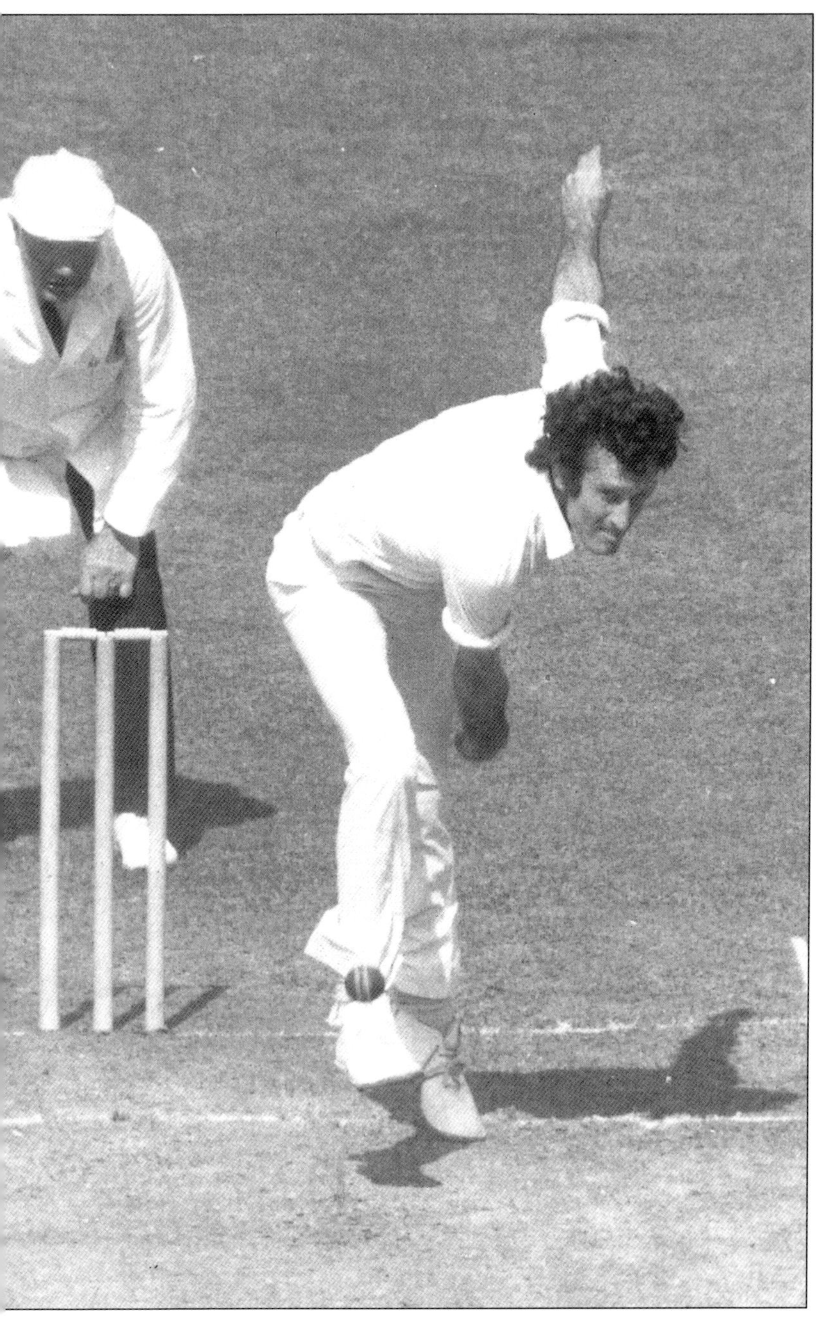

ɔhn Snow had a beautiful shoulder action, which helped him disguise his bouncer. He didn't disguise his dislike of 'baggy green' caps.

Neil Harvey (top left) with his mate Keith Miller. Harvey was a great player and the man behind my rise to the captaincy. Miller's ability and flair fired my early cricket ambitions.

Richie Benaud, a knowledgeable man on all aspects of cricket and a great help to me.

John Arlott, a genius at the microphone.

Allan Border probably gets fed up with the constant interviews that are now a way of life for an Australian captain. But for former skippers cricket commentary is a way to stay involved in the game.

A smile on the face of The Tiger. I'll bet Bill O'Reilly's not thinking about batsmen or cricket administrators.

I loved playing baseball, and in particular catching. Among other things the game taught me 'words will never hurt you'.

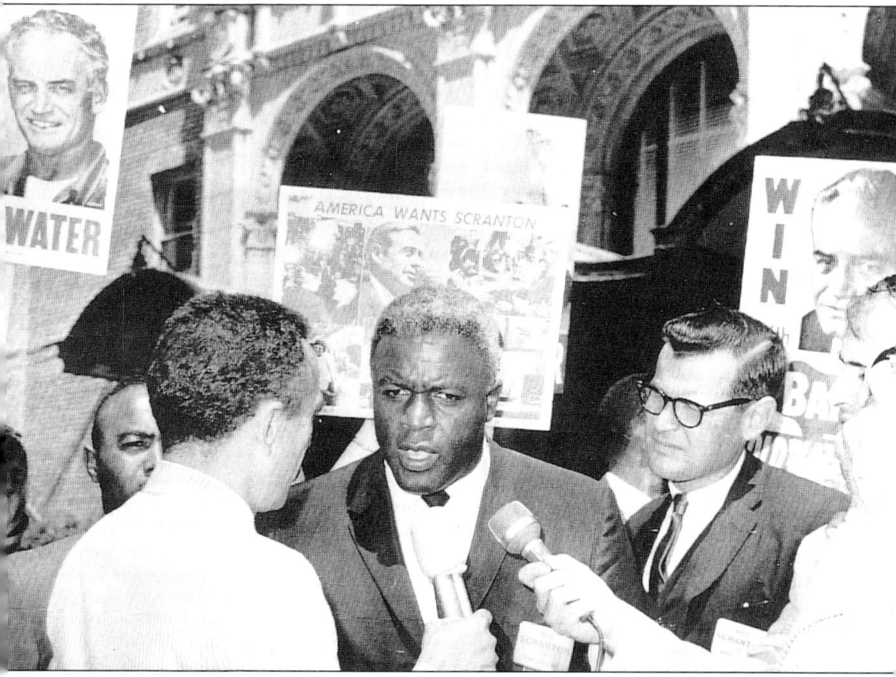

ackie Robinson broke the 'colour barrier' when he signed for the Brooklyn Dodgers
1947. In retirement he continued to fight for the rights of the underprivileged, even
'taking on' an American Presidential hopeful, Barry Goldwater.

Jack Nicklaus. Winner of more Majors than any other golfer and a champion in every sense of the word.

SLEDGING

"Subtle as a Sledgehammer."

I was there when the term 'sledging' came into being, but contrary to popular opinion, I didn't invent it.

What is sledging anyway?

Well, because of the ill-informed and poorly sourced scribblings of a few English and Australian cricket writers, it is now incorrectly defined in the Macquarie dictionary. Sledging, "n..(in cricket) the practice among bowlers and fielders of heaping abuse and ridicule on the batsman."

Fieldsmen, "heaping abuse and ridicule on the batsman," what a load of bollocks. That's where the pundits really come unstuck and display their ignorance of the game of cricket.

Any batsman (of District level, never mind Test standard) will immediately pull away if a fieldsman is chattering while he's facing up. Even if the fieldsman is giving directions to a party with an eighteen-gallon keg and an abundance of nubile women, the batsman will ask him to shut up. He may tell the fielder to write the address on a piece of paper and stick it in his pocket at the end of the over, but he'll ask for quiet while he's batting.

If that doesn't work, the batsman will then ask the umpire to deal with the problem. In most cases the umpire will be aware of the situation and act. If he's not, he'll move quickly to stop the chatter and that should be the end of the matter. However, if the fieldsman is stupid enough to continue with his inane comments, then there's a fair chance he'll be reported and dealt with by the authorities.

I was never reported during a Test match, nor on any

occasion when I was playing for Australia, and neither were any of the players under my command. I was reported in Sheffield Shield cricket, but I'll come back to that later.

I don't like the use of the term 'sledging' in reference to on-field situations. Firstly, it has become all-encompassing and that is not good for the game. Out on the field, there is either gamesmanship, a humorous aside, or there's abuse. Umpires need to differentiate and treat each case accordingly. In the first two cases the answer is to ignore it, while the latter should bring first a rebuke, then a report. And secondly, I was there the day the term 'sledging' was coined, and for me it will never have anything to do with what occurs on a cricket field. The story is worth recounting.

Grahame 'Ilbe' Corling was a fast bowler for NSW and Australia in the early sixties. Ilbe (a shortening of the Frank Ifield song title "I'll be calling you") is a likeable character who was a bit ahead of his time. Grahame used to swear in mixed company before it became fashionable.

On this occasion, the NSW team had a party in Grahame's hotel room in Adelaide. The room had quickly taken on the appearance of a London nightclub, but one of the players had to leave to attend a company function. On his return, he knocked on the door of Ilbe's room, at the same time as a waitress arrived with a tray of drinks for the party.

Corling opened the door and it became immediately obvious that what was a swinging gathering had been reduced to a drink and a discussion amongst a few teammates. "What happened to the party?" enquired the latecomer.

"It's all f...ed up," came Ilbe's straight-to-the-point reply.

Taken aback, the NSW player cast an embarrassed glance in the direction of the waitress and admonished the quickie. "Ilbe, you're as subtle as a sledgehammer."

The players who were left in the room burst out laughing and Grahame, who acquired nicknames like an autograph hunter gathers signatures, quickly became 'Percy' for the next few weeks.

Percy? Well one of the big hits at the time was "When a Man

Loves a Woman", sung by Percy Sledge. Hence the nickname, Percy. From that moment on, any cricketer in Australia who made a faux pas in front of a lady was said to be a 'sledge', or guilty of 'sledging'.

It was quite an appropriate term and was the cause of both mirth and embarrassment in its embryonic stages, but I'm afraid it has been spoilt for me by mis-use.

I can understand the ignorance of some writers, you expect that, although I was bemused by Terry Brindle's attitude. As he didn't cover the 1974-75 English tour of Australia, I asked him if he'd ever bothered to check the authenticity of the claims he was making. He said he didn't need to because it was a well-known fact. Yes, fact according to him, because other journalists had also written it without bothering to check what actually occurred.

When some of Allan Border's team members were said to have berated the Sri Lankans in 1988-89, these accusations were dismissed as being just the usual Test match banter between fast bowler and batsmen.

I can vouch for the fact that it was no different in the seventies, there was the "usual Test match banter". However, there are some people who try to portray what actually occurred as something more sinister.

A lot of sporting reputations suffer from the "If it sounds good write it regardless" mentality of some journalists. Added to that, my combative nature probably didn't help. If I had an objection I voiced it to the journalist, but having made my point, if I had any respect for him, I was then happy to continue working and socialising with the person concerned.

I never complained about a journalist's opinion of my play or my captaincy, I didn't have to read a column to find out if I'd had a bad day. However, I objected strongly to muck-raking journalism or unfair criticism of either my team or myself.

I think I also suffered from passing comment on the field, if I was unhappy with an opponent's conduct. In a lot of cases I think this was seen as an attempt by me to unsettle the opposition. Far from it. I was either defending our right as the fielding team to appeal without being glared at by the batsman concerned, or else I was objecting to a batsman trying to influence an umpire's decision by indicating whether the ball had hit the bat or the pad, depending on which best suited his chances of survival. I believe this to be a form of cheating.

Because I also was not prone to deleting expletives, the stories that circulated about what I was supposed to have said in some on-field confrontations were grossly exaggerated. Two classic examples are the Glenn Turner incident in 1973-74, and the time Geoff Boycott was run out in Adelaide in 1970-71.

I've been told on many different occasions what I was supposed to have said about Turner's wife and Boycott's girl-friend. If you have to stoop so low to win that you refer to an opponent's wife, girl-friend, race, religion or any other aspect of his private life in a derogatory way, then you shouldn't be playing cricket. I have always believed that winning the respect of the team is one of the first things a captain must do. I can't think of a quicker way to lose respect, not only as a captain, but also as a human being, than to stoop to such levels.

The *Mirror* newspaper in Sydney even headlined a story with, "What made Lennie Mad". This was in reference to racist comments I was supposed to have made in an attempt to upset Len Pascoe during a Shield match at the SCG.

One of the journalists, whose name appeared on the story, refuted the authenticity of the accusation, and Len Pascoe himself swore under oath in the courtroom that I never made any racist comment to him, either on the field or at any other time. Despite this, I still lost a defamation case. However, it did give me some satisfaction to later win an appeal against the judgement.

I was brought up to take my punishment if I did something wrong. As I mentioned earlier, I did swear at an umpire twice in Sheffield Shield matches, and on both occasions I acknowledged my guilt. In the second case I was suspended for three weeks, which I think is still the longest holiday for any player in Australia in my memory.

In 1975-76 I told the umpires to "get stuffed" after they'd

intervened while I was 'jousting' with the crowd in the outer at the MCG. Back in the dressingroom after play, I was told by two ACB officials that if I apologised the matter would be dropped. I declined to take the easy way out and said I was wrong and would accept any punishment that resulted. I got off with a reprimand.

In 1979-80, following the compromise between WSC and the ACB, I was reported by umpire Bob Marshall after he'd intervened when I told David Boon to get on with his batting and leave the appealing to us. I admitted my guilt and told the official who was gathering the evidence that I'd said, "F... off and mind your own business, you officious pommy bastard," to Marshall. I served my sentence without complaint because not only was I guilty by cricket's laws, I was also palpably wrong according to my own rule that 'You never swear at an umpire.'

Later on that same season, I was reported by an umpire in Adelaide for swearing at him. In this case I was not guilty and defended myself vigorously at a hearing chaired by Sir Donald Bradman. I was given a suspended sentence in this case, as I think some people on the ACB knew my history of owning up to what I'd done wrong and they may well have been wary of suspending me when I protested my innocence. If that was the case, then I thank those who came to my defence.

In none of those cases was I trying to unsettle an opponent. Nevertheless, on a couple of occasions, it could have appeared that that was my motive, but I swear (no pun intended) I didn't do it intentionally. On those occasions I was bored with cricket matches that were going nowhere.

My worst performance was against the Combined Universities at Oxford in 1972. A combination of boredom and anger at having lost the first Test the day before, saw me in a grumpy mood on the first day. I didn't really want to be on a cricket field the day after completing a Test, and when one University batsman commenced kicking nearly every ball with his pad and the game came to a grinding halt, I told him exactly what I thought of his display.

When we returned to the pavilion for lunch, I was sitting

with our manager Ray Steele. Feeling a little guilty, I told him how I'd blown a fuse out in the middle. Just as I was finishing my story, a University batsman named Dudley Owen-Thomas came up to the table and said, "Captain, I must apologise for my performance out there today, but I went to a ball last night and didn't get much sleep."

At first I thought he was 'taking the mickey', but then I realised he was serious. Ray, who enjoys a prank as much as the next bloke, took great delight in telling the story regularly on tour, which had the desired effect. I was the one who should have apologised and after that I endeavoured to keep my trap shut when I was bored.

Boredom never set in during a Test or a Shield match, when there was always something hanging on the end of the game, but tour matches that degenerated into pointless centre-wicket practice sessions used to get under my skin.

I overcame the problem on the 1975 tour of England by captaining only the World Cup games and the Test matches. I let either Greg or Rod Marsh lead the side in the tour games and often used to drift off down to fine leg so I was out of harm's way.

Apart from the fact that it's not true, the most annoying thing about accusations that sledging started under my captaincy is that it suggests I didn't have much confidence in my bowlers. It insinuates that I felt they weren't capable of taking wickets without 'outside assistance'. Far from it, I had the utmost confidence in the bowling attacks under my command, especially when we played England, whose journalists were the most vociferous accusers.

Many of the problems I encountered were while playing for SA. On most occasions I was simply sticking up for teammates and I make no apology for having done that. On one occasion it helped us win a Sheffield Shield.

SA needed to beat Victoria outright at the Adelaide Oval in 1975-76 to be virtually assured of winning the Shield. Chasing 364 for victory in the fourth innings, we were in trouble when Ashley Mallett joined me at the fall of the sixth wicket.

Mallett was a reasonable batsman, but he often took exception to the number of bouncers he received and started to play the hook shot in retaliation. This usually led to his rapid demise.

In Victoria's second innings I'd instructed medium-fast bowler Geoff Attenborough to bounce Victoria's opening bowler, Alan Hurst, "until I tell you to stop, or the umpire speaks to you. In the case of the latter occurring, refer him to me". I did so because Hurstie was keen on handing them out to blokes like Ashley Mallett, but wasn't too happy when he was on the receiving end.

When Mallett arrived at the crease, he copped two or three bouncers in a row from Hurst. I could see the red mist rising at the other end of the pitch and knew Rowdy was close to hooking. It was time for me to take some action if we were to have any chance of winning, because I believed a good partnership at that stage was vital.

At the completion of the over I took off with Hurst towards fine leg. On the journey, I told him if he wanted to bowl bouncers he should give himself a proper test and bowl them at me. I also threw in a few other finer points of the game and concluded by telling Alan what I would do with the bat if he bowled any more bouncers at Mallett. It was then that I realised we had company.

Umpire Tony Crafter had given chase and he seemed to be very keen on having me return to the crease and leaving Hurst to find his own way down to fine leg. On hearing this I said, "It's okay Tony, I was just telling him what would happen if he bowled any more bouncers at Mallett, and I think he's got the message." With that off my chest, the game recommenced and South Australia went on to win the match with the aid of a solid partnership between Mallett and myself.

Some people took exception to the way I took matters into my own hands, but it was a simple decision as far as I was concerned—especially in that case, where the Shield was hanging in the balance. A few years later I had a quiet chuckle to myself when I read Ray Robinson's marvellous book on

Australian captains, called *On Top Down Under*.

In the chapter on Vic Richardson he says, "Years of leading SA teams which were outgunned by NSW and Victoria sharpened his alertness for ruses to steal wins which his side was unlikely to get if matches went along in orthodox manner." Just like my bloody grandfather, eh Martin.

However, I must say that in general I believe I was a pretty quiet captain. I didn't like much chatter on the field, as it's hard enough to concentrate on the task at hand without being distracted by your own teammates. I especially hated meaningless shouts such as "car'n into 'im" from cover point as the bowler reached the top of his mark. I wanted fieldsmen who were thinking about their job, not going through the motions of showing they were a good team man by yelling innane comments. In this case, the saying "Empty vessels make the loudest noise," is apt.

Years after I'd retired from cricket, I was in Pamplona running with the bulls. Late one night I gave a rendition of the (football) coach's speech in the hall of our hotel. I adapted it for the run that morning, but basically it was a take-off of the version Ian McDonald, the ACB media relations manager, used to give each year at Melbourne's Vingt Cinq grand final lunch. David Hookes, who was trying to get some sleep, kept yelling at me to "shaaaddup and go to bed".

The next morning, one of the Englishmen in our party who was staying in the hotel made the observation that after last night he realised I must have been a vocal captain. Hookesy replied, "On the contrary. He was a very quiet captain."

It's interesting that David should have that opinion, as he played under me for SA in 1975-76 and 1979-80 and for the two seasons of WSC, during which time most of the contentious issues surrounding my captaincy arose.

I guess it all depends on who you listen to. For instance, Viv Richards said of the 1975-76 series in his book *Hitting Across the Line*, "Without doubt, it was to be the hardest, meanest cricket tour that I have ever been involved in." He wrote that in 1991, yet in his authorised biography in 1984 there isn't anything of the sort mentioned in reference to that series.

In 1985 the West Indies captain Clive Lloyd said in reference to the 1975-76 series, "I learned my lesson the hard way. Greg Chappell gave us no favours, just like elder brother Ian had played it tough but fair in the Caribbean in 1973."

Now that's a big discrepancy, similar to the difference between what I'm saying happened and what some journalists wrote. However, I think it's worth pointing out that in retirement I've never had any problems mixing socially with opponents from days gone by and reminiscing about the battles we had on the field.

One of the most regular and toughest of those opponents, Clive Lloyd, had this to say during his final tour to Australia as a player: "My career often crossed paths with the Chappell brothers and it was from them I learned the importance of toughness, aggression and fairness."

Thank you Clive. I'm sure that Martin, if he were alive, would be delighted to know that that's how we played the game. That's certainly the way we were taught to play.

A FORTUNATE LIFE

"When are you Going to get a Real Job."

A few years ago I was walking through the Channel Nine car park when I ran into successful advertising man John Singleton. He greeted me with, "When are you going to get a real job?"

When I told him I'd had a number of 'real jobs', he just rocked with laughter. My explanation that years of playing cricket, and then being a sports commentator, wasn't exactly like picking up money in the street, only sent him into more fits of laughter.

I guess it is difficult for people to understand how travelling the world playing sport can be classed as hard work. And obviously a short stint broadcasting Rugby League for a Sydney radio station had given John the wrong impression about the amount of work involved in sports broadcasting. I'm not surprised, as John was a pretty relaxed caller.

Singo was a great Newtown Jets fan when they were playing in the Sydney competition. He was calling the last grand final the Jets played in, against Parramatta at the SCG, when he came up with this gem, "It's nil-all, Newtown leading." Calling a Jets game was a labour of love for John.

To John and a lot of other people, it's pointless trying to explain that what I've been doing since I was eighteen can entail hard work. And while I believe I've worked hard during my lifetime, I must say a fairly high percentage of it has been enjoyable.

Many times people have said to me, "I'll bet you wish you were playing now, when there's more money in the game."

To which my answer is, "No. I was happy playing when I did, I had a lot of fun."

To me, I had the best of both worlds. I played in the semi-amateur days, when there was a bit more time to enjoy touring and the company of some marvellous characters. When you were around blokes like Doug Walters, Rod Marsh, Brian Taber, Garry Gilmour and Ashley Mallett, who all had active minds which were forever on the lookout for a prank, there was never a dull moment.

Then in the last couple of seasons, I enjoyed the benefits of being well paid for playing cricket. However, in that period it was often a case of play a game, throw down a beer, then pack your bag and move on to the next venue.

I don't think I would have enjoyed a full career at such a hectic pace, as I never wanted cricket to be my job. Just in case Singo thinks that is proof that I agree with his statement, I should point out that I always had a full-time job while I was playing cricket.

As a commentator, life hasn't changed much. In Australia it's usually a case of do your job and then jump on a plane and head back home, or onto the next venue. I enjoy going to the ground well before play starts to watch practice and sometimes take a wander around the ground to see what the view is like from other vantage points. That affords me the opportunity to soak up some of the atmosphere and generally discover a bit about the ground. This is something I never did as a player, hence I find it interesting as well as being helpful in my job.

The other thing I discovered that you miss out on as a player is listening to the commentators. Some people may think that's a plus. But it's not when you miss out on hearing a bloke like John Arlott.

Thanks to a young cricket fan, I had an opportunity to hear a bit of Arlott in 1972. I was immediately hooked.

This young man sent me a tape of Bob Massie's sixteen wickets at Lord's, which played such a huge part in our first victory under my captaincy. That tape contained a classic piece of Arlott commentary.

Australia were in the field at the time as Arlott described the slips cordon in his distinctive Basingstoke brogue. "At third slip Chappell the younger, Greg, wearing a long sleeved sweater and the baggy green Australian cap. At second slip Stackpole, Keith. The vice-captain has on a sleeveless sweater with his shirt buttoned at the wrists. On his head, one of those white cricketing hats that the Australians prefer. At first slip the captain. Bareheaded, the elder Chappell is sweaterless, with his shirt sleeves rolled to the elbow. Something like a progressive strip tease."

Cricket will miss John Arlott.

There's a real difference between playing and commentating when Channel Nine travels overseas to cover an Australian tour. As a player, the time in between games was taken up with practising and then relaxing on the golf course. Without the pressures that come with playing, I now find time to look around some of the places we're visiting and take in a few sights. However, one thing that never changes are the ever-present characters that make life interesting.

For instance, on our recent trip to the Caribbean, in between the One-day match and the Test at Sabina Park in Kingston, I took the opportunity to spend a couple of days relaxing at the seaside resort of Negril.

A pal of mine, Pat McGann, has a holiday place called the Beachcomber there—he told me I couldn't go back to Australia without seeing a Negril sunset. He didn't mention anything about the topless beach about twenty metres from his bar.

So it was purely with the thought of viewing a brilliant orange sunset from Ricki's cafe that I set out for Negril.

Although I left my Kingston hotel at 8:45 a.m. it was bloody near sunset by the time I reached Negril, about one hundred and eighty kilometres (as the crow flies) to the west. As I discovered, Trans Jamaica Airlines doesn't fly the same way as a crow.

I made my first mistake when I hailed a taxi from the Pegasus Hotel in Kingston. I simply asked for the airport. The driver took me to Norman Manley International and at 9:15 I joined a queue to catch the ten o'clock to Negril.

Following enquiries, I was nodded in the direction of three more lines of people before I was told that "Trans Jamaica fly Tinson Pen".

"Who is Tinson Pen?" I asked.

"Another airport, mon," was the smiling reply.

"Oh. It's just near here?" I enquired hopefully.

"No mon, thirty minutes," was the casual answer. The average Caribbeanite doesn't waste any extra effort on excess movement and they most certainly don't waste words.

Fortunately, I found a cab driver who didn't waste time, but freely described how some drivers are slack in not asking passengers which airport they want. We absolutely flew along the freeway around the harbour and thanks to some wonderful handling through the narrow streets of Old Kingston, a part of town I'd never seen on three previous trips, we arrived at Tinson Pen at 9:55. I then discovered the plane had been delayed "'til 'bout 'leven forty".

When we finally lifted off from Tinson Pen, the nine-seater roared into the air, banked left over the harbour and landed twenty seconds later at Norman Manley.

As we taxied to the terminal I was a little annoyed that I hadn't known about this stop, as I thought I could have stayed at Norman Manley and boarded with the other passengers we were obviously going to pick up. Wrong.

We dropped off one passenger. A bloody twenty minute taxi ride. A hop that, on a good day, Bob Beamon could have cleared in one bound, and we'd dropped off one passenger.

While the passenger was disembarking the pilot had to stand outside the plane. He was about a hundred and sixty centimetres tall and at three times the width of the seat, weighed in at around a hundred kilos. My mind immediately turned to The Models' hit tune, "Whooo I'm going to Barbados" and I imagined that Captain Tobias Wilcox in that song was built along similar lines. To me, our pilot was Tobias Wilcox for the rest of the trip.

As the beads of perspiration on the back of the pilot's neck increased with our speed on the tarmac, I wondered if he wasn't a frustrated grand prix driver. We must have hit two hundred kmh on the ground, a speed we didn't achieve in the air. There was a good reason for that—we were never in the air long enough.

When we banked right on take-off, I held my breath in fear that we were going to land at Tinson Pen, but no, we flew on to Port Antonio, some ten minutes away.

On pulling up near the terminal, Captain 'Tobias Wilcox' turned off the engines and over the intercom came, "Woy, yoy, ya; Woyyoy, yoy, ya," as we caught Bob Marley and the Wailers in mid-chorus of their thought-provoking hit song 'Buffalo Soldier'.

When we touched down at Port Maria, it was the amazing Professor Nuts singing Reggae on the radio. Then at Ocho Rios it was the local station RJR's talkback radio equivalent of John Laws, discussing how (now ex) Prime Minister Michael Manley once said that "if a Jamaican wanted to be a millionaire, he should remember that there are five flights a day to Miami".

Unlike the Buffalo Soldier, there was no "fighting on arrival", nor had Captain Tobias caused us to be "fighting for survival". He produced five perfect landings, the last of them at Montego Bay. However, Pat McGann must have been feeling sorry for me by then—I received the message to take my bags off at Montego Bay, as Pat was going to drive me the rest of the way.

We arrived in Negril in time to down a couple of cold Red Stripe beers in Ricki's cafe, which reminds me very much of pictures I've seen of the cliff diving spots of Acapulco, before witnessing a magnificent orange sunset. It was worth the wait.

After a couple of days relaxing at the Beachcomber I wasn't ready to head back to Kingston, but work called. Pat drove me to the Negril airport, which had a pleasant Old World charm about it after all the extra security we'd experienced en route to the Caribbean, because of the Gulf War.

The lounge was a two-room tin shed, about as big as your average suburban garage, with a bloke sitting behind a desk reading a magazine.

We'd been sitting in the front room about five minutes when a plane landed outside. "Dat de plane from Kingston?" asked a man of the cloth. "Beats me," was the prompt reply from the man in charge, as he continued to read his magazine.

As it turned out it wasn't, so I went for a walk outside.

The only thing between the lounge and the tarmac was a three strand barbed wire fence connected to a four slat wooden gate that wouldn't have kept out a French poodle. Just as well they don't fly at night around here, I thought, or my old mate Jack Newton wouldn't be the only sportsman to lose a battle with a propeller.

However, not feeling threatened in the middle of the afternoon, I opened the gate and wandered over to the fire brigade. I found two guys asleep in the cabin.

On the other side of the taxiing area, I discovered a mechanic working feverishly on an engine, whose parts were strewn all over a tarpaulin on the ground next to a twelve seater. I wasn't game to ask if this was "de plane for Kingston".

Mind you, after recently experiencing a three-hour stopover in Miami, where we had four security checks and spent the rest of the time queuing up for the privilege, I was happy enough to be in Negril.

When the plane did eventually arrive, we flew direct to Tinson Pen in around thirty-five minutes.

If ever anyone asks me, "Do you know the way to Negril?" I'll answer, "Do you want the long or the short route?"

Apart from cricket I've been fortunate through my job to be able to attend many great sporting events. I rank the Baseball World Series and the Masters golf at the head of the list.

In 1986 brother Greg and I shuttled between Shea stadium in New York and Fenway Park in Boston to follow the fortunes of the National League champion Mets and their American League counterparts, the Red Sox.

Two moments stand out in my memory. One is the occasion before game five when Ted Williams, 'the splendid splinter', walked from the back of the Fenway Park stands out onto the ground to a standing ovation. Regarded by many as the greatest hitter of all time, Ted belted a home run in his last at bat in the majors in that very same park, back in 1960.

At sixty-eight years of age he remained erect and proud throughout that long walk. I felt a tingle down my spine for the duration of the applause.

Then, in game six at Shea stadium, with the Mets down to their last out, a series of hits and then an incredible blunder from Red Sox first-baseman Billy Buckner allowed the winning run to cross home plate, and a crowd of 55,000 erupted. I haven't heard noise like that even at the MCG at its most voluble, and the Mets fans kept it up for twenty minutes. Even on the train from Flushing Station back to the city the fans were still buzzing. It was an incredible feeling.

The Masters is just the opposite. It's an opportunity to soak up the beauty of the azaleas and the dogwoods in an atmosphere of peace and quiet. Peace and quiet, that is, until Lee Trevino arrives on the scene.

I first went to Augusta in 1988. In 1989 the Mexican jumping bean led on the Thursday, after a typically adventurous 67. Knowing Lee is always good for a quote, I headed for the press conference in a hurry.

The extremely popular Trevino arrived to a tremendous ovation. As the room went quiet, Lee, who has a poor record at Augusta, said, "Well, I bet I'm the last guy you fellas expected to be interviewing."

"No," shot back one of the journos, "second last. Just before Jack Burke jun." (He was participating as the 1956 champion).

The room burst into laughter, and no one was laughing louder than Trevino. That set the mood for the funniest press conference I've ever been privileged to hear.

Lee finished it as it had started, when he was asked about bogeying the last two holes. "Well, I forgot where I was," he explained. "On these greens you can't afford to be bold and I hit both approaches at the flag. On each occasion I went through and couldn't make up and down."

"Do you find as you're getting older (Lee was due to commence playing the Seniors later that year)," asked a writer, "that you start forgetting things?"

"Yeah sure," laughed Trevino. "Why, a couple of times I've even gone to my old addresses."

With the place in an uproar, Lee bounced up from his chair and disappeared into the car park, where he changed his shoes in the back of his Toyota van. After all these years, Lee still won't change in the clubhouse because he disagrees with some of the rules at Augusta.

Lee Trevino is the most naturally funny sportsman I've met.

You sure need a sense of humour on a golf course, because that's the place where you go through a whole range of emotions.

It was at Pebble Beach in 1979, on the way home from the WSC tour of the Caribbean, that I felt most like playing golf. Ever since I became really interested in golf I had wanted to play Pebble Beach, and when I arrived I wasn't disappointed. One look from the clubhouse across the famous eighteenth fairway to the Pacific Ocean and I was ready to play.

As brother Greg, David Hookes, former Australian tennis player Ray Ruffels and I hit balls in the practice paddock, I felt this overwhelming urge to be on the course and playing. Unfortunately this didn't translate into a good round, but we had a ding-dong battle, with Ray's tremendous birdie at the last putting paid to the Chappell brothers' fightback.

My biggest disappointment came at Augusta. Although we only completed twelve holes because play was criminally slow, this wasn't the reason for the letdown. We started at the tenth tee and I was desperate to hit a decent drive at the two famous par five holes, thirteen and fifteen, which are crossed by Rae's Creek, to see if I could clear the water with my second shot. I proceeded to produce the two worst swings in the history of the game on those holes.

At the thirteenth I hit what in baseball terms would be called a 'pop-up', in the direction of first base. A fast moving fielder, if he'd come forward quickly enough, might have made the catch on the run.

So keen was I to slam one way down the fifteenth that I

employed the Guyana grip (the one they use for choke and rob), which resulted in a screaming duck hook that started turning as it passed the toe of my left shoe. Former USPGA champion Wayne Grady has the best description for that type of shot. "Two more of those and you're round a dog track."

Even on such famous holes as thirteen and fifteen at Augusta, it isn't much of a thrill when you gamble on getting across the water with your fourth shot.

Despite those setbacks, I'm still not completely disillusioned and there are a couple of things I would like to do on the golf course, as well as on the tennis court. Exactly what, I'm not going to divulge, on the grounds that they could cause me further embarrassment.

Because of the travel involved in sport, many opportunities arise to see famous sites or sights. The most exhilarating I've experienced is the trip by train through the Jungfrau in the Swiss Alps.

On the trip up through the mountain we stopped at the half-way mark and looked out on the north face of the Eiger. People ask me how I could ever want to face ninety mph fast bowling. I answer, when you're used to it and know what to look for, it's not so bad.

After seeing the Eiger, I ask how could anyone ever want to climb that sheer rock face? I guess a well-trained mountain climber would tell me, "When you're used to it and know what to do, it's not as dangerous as it looks." Each to his own. I'm just glad Martin bought me a cricket bat when I was first able to walk, not climbing boots.

When we reached the top there was a low cloud (not that low, I guess, because the Jungfrau is 4158m high) which reduced visibility to virtually nil. There was nothing to do but visit the bar and hope.

With about fifteen minutes remaining before we had to catch the train back to Grindewald, the cloud lifted and we had a magnificent view right down the valley. The people in the valley looked like busy little ants, and the brilliant whiteness of the snow gave me a feeling of being in another world. My wife,

Barbara, aptly described the scene as "just like climbing out of a spaceship that has landed on the moon".

It has indeed been a fortunate life. Any regrets? Just one.

When I was around fourteen years old, I woke up in the middle of a dream-filled sleep. I went and asked my father if I could go to America and play baseball. Martin told me to forget such thoughts and concentrate on my cricket. Father was right. However, I still have the odd day when I wonder what it would have been like to play baseball in America.

SOME PEOPLE I ADMIRE

"Stuff the Goddam Bat Right Up Your Ass."

As a kid I grew up practising, playing, watching and listening to sport. I still have vague memories of the Ashes Test at Adelaide Oval in 1950-51 and of listening to the 1952 Olympics in Helsinki on the pride of the Chappell household, the brand new Scharnberg Strauss radiogram.

I was seven years old when Dad first took me to watch Australia play England at the Adelaide Oval. Despite a double century from Arthur Morris and Len Hutton carrying his bat for 156, the thing I remember about that game was Keith Miller hurdling his bat. Miller was sliding his bat towards the crease to avoid being run out, when the toe of the bat dug into the turf and stopped abruptly. If Keith hadn't reacted quickly and athletically he could well have been skewered by his own bat.

There is a good reason why I remember Miller. He was my idol, and at the Adelaide Oval that day Dad encouraged me to "watch Miller, look at what he does".

Keith Ross Miller was born fifteen days after Dad. He served in the Air Force, the same as Martin did, and as in our family, Keith sired only boys. I think deep down he was my father's idol as well.

When I first went to England to play in the Lancashire League in 1963, I recall talking with an Australian friend of mine, Ray Hogan, about Keith. I had discovered that Ray was in the NSW practice squad while Miller was still playing and I pumped Ray for information. I was a very happy nineteen-year-old when Ray told me, "Keith Miller is one of the most generous men you'd meet. If he had a hundred quid in his pocket, he'd give you ninety-nine if you needed it."

As we drove to a benefit game, Ray told me that someone had asked Keith if he'd play in a cricket match, and Miller, who had been retired for half a dozen years at the time, said he didn't play anymore. Then the guy told Keith it was for charity, so he went out and bought a new pair of cricket boots and played in the match.

The first time I met Keith Miller was on the tour of South Africa in 1966-67. It was a wonderful bonus when a friend of mine in Johannesburg, Martin Shein, invited me to play golf at Bryanston, near the Kyalami grand prix track, and then informed me that Keith would be playing in our four.

That day, Keith played like he was in a hurry to get back to the bar. He hit 'em on the run, but the highlight of the day for me was travelling back to Johannesburg in Martin's car with Keith Miller. In later years, I had reason to recall something Keith told me, about writing for newspapers, on that car trip. He said, with his characteristic clearing of his throat, "Ahem, always remember who you're writing for, son. You write for the editor, not to please the players."

In 1972, on my first tour as captain of Australia, we were at the British Sportsmans Club in Tottenham Court Road, when Keith came rushing up to me, shook hands and said, "I'm glad they made you captain, ahem. Good luck and by the way, don't take any notice of anything I write about you."

With that he disappeared into the crowd, almost as quickly as he'd materialised.

Years later, Dennis Lillee was angry with Keith over something he'd written. I told Dennis about Keith's philosophy on writing and suggested he make a point of having a chat with him some time. Dennis sought out Miller and afterwards he told me it was an enjoyable experience, as well as a profitable one. Dennis had picked up a couple of tips on bowling.

No matter who he was writing for, deep down Keith Miller was a keen follower of Australia's fortunes. He was also generous in his praise, as I found out on a hot steamy day in

Guyana in 1973.

Opening bowlers Max Walker and Jeff Hammond had just put in a mammoth stint at the Bourda ground to put us in a winning position. After trailing by twenty-five on the first innings, their lionhearted performance had the West Indies struggling at eight down for just under a hundred.

As we left the ground for lunch, the team stood back and applauded Walker and Hammond from the field. As I walked up the stairs of the old wooden pavilion, a hand suddenly reached through the crowd and grabbed me by the arm. "Tell Walker and Hammond, ahem, I'm bloody proud of them," said a voice, and then he was gone. I hardly had time to recognise that it was Australia's finest allrounder dishing out this accolade.

I can tell you Max and Jeff were mighty tired, but extremely pleased to receive such praise from a former great.

As a kid I had Keith Miller up on a pedestal and I'm delighted to be able to say that I've never had reason to do anything but look up to the man.

When I was young I didn't really have a bowling action of my own, I was too busy imitating the actions of the Test players. However, the one I imitated best involved a flick of the hair off the forehead, before taking a couple of short quick steps and then settling into a shoulder-shrugging run to the wicket—just like Keith Miller.

Not long after Miller's retirement, I made the first eleven at school and realised that I had to settle into one style of bowling. I had been a leg-spinner at primary school and then had tried my hand at medium-pace and off-spin. Around 1958-59 I went back to leg-spin bowling, the same season that Richie Benaud became captain of Australia.

I didn't imitate Richie's action, except in lighter moments in the nets, but I used to wear my shirt open at the chest when I was in the field. I only stopped doing that when I heard about skin cancer.

Ironically, my first Shield match for South Australia was as twelfth man against New South Wales, led by Richie Benaud. Thanks to Garry Sobers' incredible 251 that I talked about earlier, SA pulled off a rare victory over the all-conquering NSW line-up in that match.

I had to field on the final day and when SA won, Richie was unconquered. Instead of walking off first as the batsmen normally do, Richie stood back and allowed the victorious team to leave the ground to generous applause. However, as twelfth man, I didn't think I should be walking off ahead of Australia's captain and I hung back, quite happy to follow Richie and Doug Ford, the other NSW batsman.

"After you, Ian," said Richie as he waved his bat to indicate that I should go ahead, and I floated off the ground, happy as a sand boy. That was my first direct contact with Richie, although I do recall one other thing he said in that game.

That season, 1961-62, was the last of NSW's nine Shield victories on the trot, so they weren't used to being on the receiving end. However, Sobey had dished it out during his double-century and I remember Richie walking into the SA dressingroom after a long day in the field chasing leather.

"Sit down, Benords," said SA skipper Les Favell, with a big grin on his face. "Now you know what it's like to feel rooted."

"Who's rooted?" replied Richie, as he forced a grin and then with an exaggerated motion, slumped into the chair Les had pushed towards him.

As captain, Les was largely responsible for the disappearance of any inferiority complexes amongst the SA players. He was the most confident player I've ever met, and I had an early lesson on his thoughts about bowlers.

On my arrival in the State side, Les told me, "You're here to be seen and not 'eard, son." So, when Richie first came on to bowl in that match, I whispered quietly to Neil Hawke, "Geez, it must be difficult batting against this bloke."

Before Hawkeye had a chance to reply, Les piped up, "Like a red rag to a bull, son. Just jump down the track and 'it 'im back over his head."

I didn't pursue that policy when I eventually faced Richie, but I did have the good fortune to make my first first-class hundred against New South Wales.

After that innings Richie again came into the SA dressingroom. This time he approached wicket-keeper Barry Jarman and asked, "Is young Chappell a smart arse?"

Worried that I'd said something to Richie in the middle (if I had it would have only been to call him Mr. Benaud), Jarman asked, "Why?"

"Because the whole time he was batting, he kept grinning at me," replied Benaud.

Relieved, Jarman burst out laughing and said, "Oh that. He grits his teeth when he's batting and it just looks like he's grinning."

Martin would have been proud of me. He was always telling me to "grit your teeth, son, and get your head down".

Richie was obviously happy with Jar's explanation, because he sent me a brand new Gray-Nicolls bat when I arrived at Ramsbottom to play in the Lancashire League, just a few months afterwards.

That was the first time, but by no means the last, that Richie Benaud helped me. On most occasions when I've needed some advice, whether it be on cricket, captaincy, business or just life, he is the person I turn to. His advice has always been to the point and full of commonsense.

I always enjoy Richie's company, especially on the rare occasions when I take a few dollars off him on the golf course, and he still says, "After you, Ian," whenever I offer him the front seat of the car.

Richie has often said he really became a good leg-spinner after having a long chat with Bill 'Tiger' O'Reilly in 1953. Part of Tiger's advice was to avoid giving runs away to batsmen. Having read Bill's thoughts on his arch-enemy the willow-wielder, I realise now it was a policy that he not only preached, but also pursued.

Tiger may not have given much away on the field, but off the field he has provided me with many hours of pleasure in the press box and while chatting over a cold glass of his favourite brew.

The first time I really got to know Bill was on New Year's

Eve before we played New Zealand at the MCG in 1973-74. After a fair amount of chiacking, a golf match had been arranged for that day, in which Jack Fingleton and Keith Butler (a cricket writer with the Adelaide *Advertiser*) played Rodney Marsh and myself. Tiger came along just for the ride as he'd retired from golf, but he was an old mate of the secretary at the Victoria Golf Club, the cricketer's friend, Jack Merrick.

On the trip to the course I was told how O'Reilly's retirement had come about. As a fifteen handicapper, he'd had a bad day at Mere Golf Club in Lancashire on the 1938 tour. At the end of the round he took off his golf shoes, threw them into the lake and said, "That's it. I'll never play this bloody game again."

Tiger is what you might call strong-willed. He's never hit a golf ball since.

After an enjoyable game of golf (which we won by instigating a feud between Fingo and Butler), we were stuck at the golf club because we couldn't make contact with a taxi company to drive us back to Melbourne.

When we realised we had no hope of getting a cab, we then inveigled Jack Merrick into letting us join the black tie crowd dining at the club. After an entertaining evening, we arrived back at the journo's pub at around 12.30. Fingo and Butler had alighted from the taxi and Tiger was halfway out, when Rodney said, "Where are we going for a drink now?"

Like a shot Bill was back in the car and it was only after Jack half cajoled and half dragged him out of the cab, that Rodney and I were able to proceed to our hotel. At the time Tiger was nearing seventy, but age was never a barrier to Tiger.

He once told me that as a young leg-spinner he came home whingeing about a bad back after bowling a lot of overs on a hot day in the bush. His father heard him out for a few seconds and then said, "Son, would you like to know how not to get a bad back, so you don't have to walk around with a bit of a stoop? And would you like to know how not to get arthritis, so your fingers and knees don't give you hell on cold days?"

"Sure, Dad," said young Tiger, eager for the remedy.

"Die before you reach thirty-five," was his father's reply.

Like father, like son, Bill was always practical, but he ignored the advice to die young.

He was seventy-eight years of age when I joined him in the bar at the Perth Sheraton for a couple of much needed quiet beers, after copping a haranguing outside the hotel from some guy who had it in for me. We were halfway through the first beer, when the guy who had made all the threats suddenly appeared in the bar. He marched up to me, continued his tirade of abuse, and ended it by suggesting we should go outside and sort it out.

"If you want a fight, I'll accommodate you," said Tiger, taking off his cloth cap and plonking his beer on the table. He almost had his sports jacket off as well before Dick Tucker, a cricket writer with the *Mirror*, convinced Tiger there was no need to fight the bloke, because the security guards would deal with him.

One of the most engaging things about Tiger, whether he's talking cricket, telling a story or dispensing some of his homespun philosophy, is the fire that forever burns brightly in his belly.

On retiring as a player, I made a point of trying to spend a bit of time talking with Tiger during each Test. You never knew what you might learn, and it was always interesting and colourful. I remember his last day in the press box, which appropriately was at his beloved SCG.

Tiger was into his eighties by this time. I had asked our producer if I could interview O'Reilly in his favourite seat in the press box. This seat was the same one he had occupied for over forty years.

The producer agreed to my request, but it took me an age to set up the interview. Tiger was busy doing numerous radio and press interviews and it was well after lunch before I could catch him. Bill agreed to my request, but said it had to be done before the end of the tea break, as he had to sit down and write his column. He always wrote in longhand in one of those lined exercise books.

We duly did the interview and at the end I told Bill, "What we'll miss most of all, Tiger, is your company in the press box."

"From the look in your eyes, son," said Bill, "I can tell you mean that and I thank you." With that Tiger reached for his pen and notebook.

I was extremely interested to see how his column turned out after such a busy day. When I read it in the *Sydney Morning Herald* the next morning it was a gem. Tiger to a T. I have kept a copy and I read it occasionally. It reminds me of a man in excess of eighty, who retired while he was still at his peak.

Jack Nicklaus was just coming to his peak when I started to play golf seriously, on my first overseas tour. Being in South Africa for nearly six months meant there was plenty of opportunity to play and loads of good courses to tackle. In 1966-67, Sunday was still a rest day on a cricket tour and there were no One-day Internationals to play.

As my interest in golf grew, I started to follow the fortunes of Nicklaus, because of the prodigious distance he hit the ball. I got my first look at Nicklaus (who was then known as 'Ohio Fats' for the excess weight he carried) playing at Adelaide's Kooyonga Golf Club in the 1965 Australian Open. Jack had won the Open for the first of six times in 1964, and I set out with a big gallery to follow him for the first round. However, news came through that Gary Player was running hot, and my sense of history took over from my sense of loyalty.

I deserted Jack in time to catch the man in black hit an iron to the ninth green and then make a long eagle putt to send him out in 29. Sensing the opportunity to witness a sub-sixty round I stuck with Player, but he 'blew out' to 33 on the back nine and shot a 62.

I never 'deserted' Jack again, but in 1979 on a visit to the Mony tournament at the La Costa course in Carlsbad, California, I did follow Jack Newton instead of Nicklaus. That is, I followed 'Newt the beaut' for four holes and Nicklaus for fourteen.

Newt and I were always a jinx on one another's sporting endeavours. Whenever he came to a cricket ground I invariably got out straight away, and when I followed him on the golf course he made bogeys.

However, I decided at La Costa this was all too stupid for words and that there was really no jinx. While I watched, Newton bogeyed the first and the second. If it wasn't a jinx, Jack was playing some mighty uncharacteristic golf, so I headed for the Golden Bear's group.

When I got to the last with Nicklaus I looked at the leader board and saw that Newt was two under after sixteen (four under since I'd left him). I dashed off and reached Newton's group in time to see him bogey seventeen and eighteen, to finish at even par.

To show there were no hard feelings, Jack took me into the players' lounge and introduced me to Nicklaus, Tom Watson and Lee Trevino. At the time we had just finished playing World Series Cricket and Nicklaus was making substantial changes to Sydney's Australian Golf Club, so we talked about Kerry Packer's influence on those two projects.

It was through Kerry's television interests and my job with *Wide World of Sports* that I was able to link Jack Nicklaus and Jack Newton a few years later. Unfortunately, it was to get a message to Newt in an attempt to boost his morale after he had an horrific accident with an aeroplane propeller on his way home from a football match.

When I got through to Barbara Nicklaus, she told me Jack was in Canada for their Open. She asked after Jack Newton and then told me that if I rang her husband's hotel at nine o'clock their time I'd catch him.

When I got through to Nicklaus, I told him that I wanted Jack's mates from the US Tour to send a message via television to him in Australia. Nicklaus was most concerned about Newton's health and said, "I know what you want, just tell the local television crew to be by the first tee at eight o'clock tomorrow morning and I'll organise the rest."

True to his word, the Golden Bear had everyone lined up and the messages came through. His wife also sent flowers and a message to Jack's wife, Jacquie Newton.

Displaying typical sportsman's humour at a time of much

trauma, Nicklaus said in his message, "Hi Jackson, I hope you're better soon. I didn't realise going to the football could be such a tough deal."

I have followed Nicklaus' golf career closely and admired his play. I believe he's the best competitor I've seen, and I can't think of anyone from any sport who can match him for success over such a long period. I've also had the good fortune through my job to come in contact with him on quite a few occasions off the course. He has always been helpful and generous with his time and a champion in every sense of the word.

All through my life I've had an equal love of cricket and baseball. I love reading about the game of baseball and its players. I enjoy watching the game whenever I can, and one of my fondest sporting memories is of seeing the 1986 World Series between the New York Mets and the Boston Red Sox.

Apart from not having had the opportunity to play baseball as much as I would have liked, my one regret is that I didn't see Jackie Robinson play. Jackie broke the colour bar in 1947 when he became the first black man to play in the major leagues.

Jackie had a distinguished career with the Brooklyn Dodgers and retired just before they moved to Los Angeles for the 1958 season. I became interested in Robinson as much for his intelligence in adversity as for his achievements as a player.

In 1987 we ran a story about Jackie Robinson's career on *Wide World of Sports* and I had the pleasure of introducing the segment. This is what I said: "Forty years ago this season, Jack Roosevelt Robinson became the first black man to play baseball in the American Major Leagues. What Jackie Robinson did in his ten seasons with the Brooklyn Dodgers is one of the great sporting achievements. As a pioneer for his race, Jackie not only had to succeed as a player, which he did admirably, but he had to put up with racist comments and vicious attempts to injure him from the bigots, who at the time were as common in the game of baseball as safe hits.

Off the field, Jackie Robinson had to endure the threats of some teams not to play against the Dodgers if he was included in the line-up and the indignity of being housed in different hotels to his white teammates. The Jackie Robinson story is one of skill, bravery and the special intelligence required to overcome ignorant, but powerful people. The 1987 American Baseball season has been dedicated to the memory of Jackie Robinson, a great man who died in 1972."

When I finished, my co-commentator Mike Gibson said, "Good introduction." I was pleased Gibbo thought so, because as a writer himself, I felt he was recognising how much feeling had gone into that piece.

To better understand Jackie Robinson's accomplishments, you first should know how competitive he was as a ball player. In Roger Kahn's book, *The Boys of Summer*, Leo 'The Lip' Durocher, a player/manager with the Dodgers who had a spiky relationship with Robinson, said, "Ya want a guy that comes to play. This guy (Robinson) didn't just come to play. He come to beat ya. He come to stuff the goddam bat right up your ass."

Despite being one of the most competitive athletes you'd ever wish to meet on a playing field, for two seasons Jackie Robinson was cursed, spiked and racially abused every time he stepped on a major league baseball diamond, without once retaliating. When the Dodgers' manager Branch Rickey eventually cleared the way for Jackie to play in 1947, he had made him promise that he wouldn't do a thing to jeopardise this ground-breaking move. Jackie Robinson kept his promise.

As Roger Kahn so eloquently put it, "He (Robinson) bore the burden of a pioneer and the weight made him more strong."

However, as Peter Golenbock reports in his book *Bums*, things changed after Jackie had been in the majors for two seasons. At spring training before the 1949 season, Jackie told his Dodger teammates, "There are a lot of players in the league who have knocked me down, spiked me, done these things to me and I put up with it. But I am convinced I am a major league ballplayer and from this point on, I take nothing from no one, on this team or on any other team, not from umpires or anyone else."

Having established the rules on the field, he started to agitate off the field as well. For a start, he wanted to be able to eat with his white teammates in the dining room of all hotels, rather than stay in his room, as he had to do in some establishments.

Jackie Robinson had to fight for every advance, both on and off the field. Without his bravery and intelligent approach to a highly inflammable situation, changes would have been a lot slower in coming. Because his heroic efforts were occurring in the glare of the spotlight on the national pastime, it also had an influence on what happened in everyday life in the USA.

Sadly, a successful career fighting for a cause had it's downside for Jackie Robinson. When his eldest son Jackie jun. was charged with possessing drugs and a rifle, a television reporter asked, "Were you aware that he had certain problems, Mr. Robinson?"

His answer told the sad story of many a dedicated sportsman. "He quit high school. He joined the Army. He fought in Vietnam and he was wounded. We lost him somewhere. I've had more effect on other people's kids than on my own."

It's not surprising. You see, Jack junior was born in 1946, the year before Jack senior became the first black man to play major league baseball. Even a man as great as Jackie Robinson couldn't successfully fight a war on all fronts.

I think the most important thing I've discovered about successful athletes is that they are themselves. They have got to know themselves well and they don't try to be anything else.

If you ever need a good example of why, as a sportsman, you should never try to be anything but yourself, it came during the 1992 US Open golf tournament at Pebble Beach.

England's Nick Faldo, who has been unfairly painted by the media as a colourless, but highly successful, competitor, was falling back after having made a challenge for the title. During the first round he'd hit a ball into a tree at the sixteenth and had climbed the tree in an attempt to locate the ball. After unsuccessfully shaking the tree for a minute or so, he cried out in a perfect Tarzan imitation, "Where's Jane?" This brought howls of laughter from the crowd and much applause on his arrival back on land.

In the final round, his challenge fell away because he was unable to convert good shots into birdies, as his putting touch deserted him. Too late, he finally holed a monster at that same sixteenth hole and did a bit of a sashay to the hole as he went to collect his ball. Once again this brought howls of delight from the crowd.

"What's this," exclaimed an indignant American ABC television commentator, Jim McKay, "the new funny Faldo?"

A case of damned if you do and damned if you don't.

Early in my career I told someone, "Fifty percent of the people will like you and fifty percent won't and I don't think you can do much to alter the odds."

Since then, I haven't seen anything to make me change my mind. I still think the only way to live is to do your best, learn as much as you can along the way, and be honest with everyone, including yourself. But above all, be yourself.